D1611651

Richard T. Spence
Diana M. DiNitto
Shulamith Lala Ashenberg Straussner
Editors

Neurobiology of Addictions: Implications for Clinical Practice

Neurobiology of Addictions: Implications for Clinical Practice has been co-published simultaneously as *Journal of Social Work Practice in the Addictions,* Volume 1, Number 3 2001.

Pre-publication
REVIEWS,
COMMENTARIES,
EVALUATIONS . . .

"**E** xceptional . . . a needed resource on this essential topic. From the neuroplasticity theory of dynamic neuronal connections, to brain chemistry's effects on emotions, to neurobiologic theory linkages on both psychosocial treatment and pharmacotherapies, this volume sounds the alarm–that social workers need to integrate this key knowledge base. AN EXCELLENT SUPPLEMENT TO CHEMICAL DEPENDENCY TEXTS, many of which lack depth on neurobiologic issues."

Morris Burnham, PhD, LCSW
University Foundation
Assistant Professor of Social Work
The University of Tennessee
at Chattanooga

More Pre-publication
REVIEWS, COMMENTARIES, EVALUATIONS . . .

"**S**HOULD HAVE A PLACE IN ANY SOCIAL WORK ADDICTIONS COURSE. In addition, because significant numbers of clients in most human service settings have substance use disorders, this book SHOULD BE INCORPORATED INTO OTHER KEY COURSES in the social work curriculum, including those in health, mental health, disability, child welfare, and human behavior. Also AN INVALUABLE RESOURCE FOR EXPERIENCED PRACTITIONERS."

Nancy J. Smyth, PhD, MSW, CASAC
Associate Professor and Associate Dean
University at Buffalo
School of Social Work

"**T**O SAY THIS VOLUME IS A MUST FOR EVERY SOCIAL WORKER IN THE ADDICTIONS FIELD IS AN UNDERSTATEMENT. It addresses a critical void by putting the biological back into the biopsychosocial approach. This is an excellent collection of well written, relevant, understandable articles which provide comprehensive exposure to such key concerns as the neurobiological causes of addiction and the impact of drugs and alcohol on the brain throughout the life cycle. THIS BOOK SHOULD BE INCORPORATED AS REQUIRED READING IN EVERY SOCIAL WORK COURSE ON ADDICTIONS as well as included in every social worker's professional library."

Ann A. Abbott, PhD, LCSW
Professor and MSW Program Director
West Chester University
Pennsylvania

The Haworth Social Work Practice Press
An Imprint of The Haworth Press, Inc.

Neurobiology of Addictions: Implications for Clinical Practice

Neurobiology of Addictions: Implications for Clinical Practice has been co-published simultaneously as *Journal of Social Work Practice in the Addictions,* Volume 1, Number 3 2001.

The *Journal of Social Work Practice in the Addictions*[TM] Monographic "Separates"

Below is a list of "separates," which in serials librarianship means a special issue simultaneously published as a special journal issue or double-issue *and* as a "separate" hardbound monograph. (This is a format which we also call a "DocuSerial.")

"Separates" are published because specialized libraries or professionals may wish to purchase a specific thematic issue by itself in a format which can be separately cataloged and shelved, as opposed to purchasing the journal on an on-going basis. Faculty members may also more easily consider a "separate" for classroom adoption.

"Separates" are carefully classified separately with the major book jobbers so that the journal tie-in can be noted on new book order slips to avoid duplicate purchasing.

You may wish to visit Haworth's Website at . . .

http://www.HaworthPress.com

. . . to search our online catalog for complete tables of contents of these separates and related publications.

You may also call 1-800-HAWORTH (outside US/Canada: 607-722-5857), or Fax 1-800-895-0582 (outside US/Canada: 607-771-0012), or e-mail at:

getinfo@haworthpressinc.com

Neurobiology of Addictions: Implications for Clinical Practice, edited by Richard T. Spence, PhD, MSSW, Diana M. DiNitto, PhD and Shulamith Lala Ashenberg Straussner, DSW, CAS (Vol. 1, No. 3, 2001). *Presents the neurobiological theories of addiction in a psychosocial context and connects the theoretical information with practical applications.*

Neurobiology of Addictions: Implications for Clinical Practice

Richard T. Spence
Diana M. DiNitto
Shulamith Lala Ashenberg Straussner
Editors

Neurobiology of Addictions: Implications for Clinical Practice has been co-published simultaneously as *Journal of Social Work Practice in the Addictions,* Volume 1, Number 3 2001.

The Haworth Social Work Practice Press
An Imprint of
The Haworth Press, Inc.
New York • London • Oxford

Published by

The Haworth Social Work Practice Press, 10 Alice Street, Binghamton, NY 13904-1580 USA

The Haworth Social Work Practice Press is an imprint of The Haworth Press, Inc., 10 Alice Street, Binghamton, NY 13904-1580 USA.

Neurobiology of Addictions: Implications for Clinical Practice has been co-published simultaneously as *Journal of Social Work Practice in the Addictions*, Volume 1, Number 3 2001.

Cover design by Thomas J. Mayshock Jr.

Library of Congress Cataloging-in-Publication Data

Neurobiology of addictions: implications for clinical practice / editors, Richard T. Spence, Diane M. DiNitto, Shulamith Lala Ashenberg Straussner
     p. cm.
    Includes bibliographical references and index.
    ISBN 0-7890-1666-4 (hard: alk. paper) – ISBN 0-7890-1667-2 (pbk.: alk. paper)
    1. Substance abuse–Physiological aspects–Congresses. 2. Drug abuse–Physiological aspects–Congresses. 3. Brain–Effect of drugs on–Congresses. 4. Neurobiology–Congresses. 5. Neuropsychopharmacology–Congresses. I. Spence, Richard T. (Richard Thomas), 1943- II. DiNitto, Diana M. III. Straussner, Shulamith Lala Ashenberg.
    RC563.2.N48 2002
    616.86'07–dc21   2002017180

Indexing, Abstracting & Website/Internet Coverage

This section provides you with a list of major indexing & abstracting services. That is to say, each service began covering this periodical during the year noted in the right column. Most Websites which are listed below have indicated that they will either post, disseminate, compile, archive, cite or alert their own Website users with research-based content from this work. (This list is as current as the copyright date of this publication.)

Abstracting, Website/Indexing Coverage . . . . Year When Coverage Began

- *Alcohol Research. For more information visit us at:*
  <http://www.voeding.tno.nl/alcohol-research> 2001

- *CINAHL (Cumulative Index to Nursing & Allied Health*
  Literature), in print, EBSCO, and SilverPlatter, Data-Star,
  and PaperChase. (Support materials include Subject Heading List,
  Database Search Guide, and instructional video). 2001

- *CNPIEC Reference Guide: Chinese National Directory*
  of Foreign Periodicals 2000

- *Criminal Justice Abstracts* 2001

- *Family & Society Studies Worldwide*
  <www.nisc.com> 2000

- *FINDEX <www.publist.com>* 2001

- *Gay & Lesbian Abstracts provides comprehensive & in-depth*
  coverage of the world's GLBT literature compiled by NISC &
  published on the Internet & CD-ROM
  <www.nisc.com> 2001

- *IBZ International Bibliography of Periodical Literature* 2001

- *Index to Periodical Articles Related to Law* 2001

(continued)

*Special Bibliographic Notes related to special journal issues
(separates) and indexing/abstracting:*

- indexing/abstracting services in this list will also cover material in any "separate" that is co-published simultaneously with Haworth's special thematic journal issue or DocuSerial. Indexing/abstracting usually covers material at the article/chapter level.
- monographic co-editions are intended for either non-subscribers or libraries which intend to purchase a second copy for their circulating collections.
- monographic co-editions are reported to all jobbers/wholesalers/approval plans. The source journal is listed as the "series" to assist the prevention of duplicate purchasing in the same manner utilized for books-in-series.
- to facilitate user/access services all indexing/abstracting services are encouraged to utilize the co-indexing entry note indicated at the bottom of the first page of each article/chapter/contribution.
- this is intended to assist a library user of any reference tool (whether print, electronic, online, or CD-ROM) to locate the monographic version if the library has purchased this version but not a subscription to the source journal.
- individual articles/chapters in any Haworth publication are also available through the Haworth Document Delivery Service (HDDS).

Neurobiology of Addictions: Implications for Clinical Practice

CONTENTS

ABOUT THE EDITORS

Richard T. Spence, PhD, ACSW, LMSW, LCDC, is a Research Scientist in the Center for Social Work Research at the University of Texas at Austin. Dr. Spence is Director of the Addiction Technology Transfer Center located at the University of Texas. He served for 16 years as director of research at the Texas Commission of Alcohol and Drug Abuse; under his direction, the research group produced more than 60 research publications. Dr. Spence has served as principal investigator or research director for 10 major federal research and demonstration projects with budgets totaling more than $30 million. He has also served as a member of the Washington staff of the National Institute on Drug Abuse and the National Institute on Alcohol Abuse and Alcoholism.

Diana M. DiNitto, PhD, ACSW, LMSW-ACP, AAC, is Cullen Trust Centennial Professor of Alcohol Studies and Education and a Distinguished Teaching Professor at the University of Texas at Austin. Dr. DiNitto teaches courses on substance abuse and dependence, social welfare policy, and research. She is the author or co-author of numerous books, articles, and chapters on substance use disorders, women's issues (especially sexual assault), and social welfare policy. Dr. DiNitto serves on the Board of Directors of the Texas Research Society on Alcoholism.

Shulamith Lala Ashenberg Straussner, DSW, CAS, is Full Professor at New York University's Shirley M. Ehrenkranz School of Social Work and is Coordinator of the post-master's program in the treatment of alcohol and drug-abusing clients. She has been involved in the field of addictions for more than 25 years. Dr. Straussner has taught in Israel and Russia as well as in the United States. She is the author or co-author of numerous publications and is the founding editor of the new *Journal of Social Work Practice in the Addictions.* Her professional affiliations and credits are too numerous to list. She maintains a private practice in psychoanalytic psychotherapy and couples counseling.

Preface

Few social workers today have enough understanding of neurobiology of addictions to make an informed decision as to its value in the treatment of addicted clients. Thus the importance of understanding this rapidly growing knowledge cannot be over-emphasized.

It is therefore a pleasure to be able to devote a special collection to this topic, and a privilege to have the leadership of Drs. Richard Spence and Diana DiNitto to guide the publication of this very special volume.

Shulamith Lala Ashenberg Straussner, DSW, CAS
New York, NY

[Haworth co-indexing entry note]: "Preface." Straussner, Shulamith Lala Ashenberg. Co-published simultaneously in *Journal of Social Work Practice in the Addictions* (The Haworth Social Work Practice Press, an imprint of The Haworth Press, Inc.) Vol. 1, No. 3, 2001, p. xv; and: *Neurobiology of Addictions: Implications for Clinical Practice* (ed: Richard T. Spence, Diana M. DiNitto, and Shulamith Lala Ashenberg Straussner) The Haworth Social Work Practice Press, an imprint of The Haworth Press, Inc., 2001, p. xi. Single or multiple copies of this article are available for a fee from The Haworth Document Delivery Service [1-800-342-9678, 9:00 a.m. - 5:00 p.m. (EST). E-mail address: getinfo@haworthpressinc.com].

Introduction

This special collection is a result of an invitational Summit on Social Work and the Neurobiology of Addictions hosted by the School of Social Work at the University of Texas at Austin on June 11-13, 2000. The Summit arose from a desire for improved linkage of social work practice, education, and research with advances in basic science research in understanding the neurobiological bases of addictions. Summit participants considered recent research on addictions and neurobiology with an eye toward bridging the gulf that exists between advancements in addictions research at the molecular neurobiological level and the practice of social workers in preventing substance abuse and treating clients who are chemically dependent.

Why was this summit on the neurobiology of addictions needed? In spite of a spirit of optimism among scientists arising from the expansion of knowledge in neurobiology, there is a "disconnect" between science and practice. Practitioners who are impatient for improved technology to use in their interventions feel this disconnection. Scientists who observe clinical reluctance to integrate new findings into practice also feel it. Professionals within the two domains of science and practice use different languages, employ different theoretical frameworks, and have little interaction. This conference was a step toward a more effective working relationship between them.

NEUROSCIENCE AND ADDICTIONS TREATMENT

Research has led us to a new understanding of addiction as a brain disease. During the past decade, rapid gains have been made in knowledge of how drugs affect the brain and how chronic use changes the brain in ways that per-

[Haworth co-indexing entry note]: "Introduction." Spence, Richard T. and Diana M. DiNitto. Co-published simultaneously in *Journal of Social Work Practice in the Addictions* (The Haworth Social Work Practice Press, an imprint of The Haworth Press, Inc.) Vol. 1, No. 3, 2001, pp. 1-6; and: *Neurobiology of Addictions: Implications for Clinical Practice* (ed: Richard T. Spence, Diana M. DiNitto, and Shulamith Lala Ashenberg Straussner) The Haworth Social Work Practice Press, an imprint of The Haworth Press, Inc., 2001, pp. 1-6. Single or multiple copies of this article are available for a fee from The Haworth Document Delivery Service [1-800-342-9678, 9:00 a.m. - 5:00 p.m. (EST). E-mail address: getinfo@haworthpressinc.com].

1

sist even after use ends. Scientists have identified the major receptors for abused drugs, developed methods to manipulate receptor systems, and have made progress in elaborating many of the biochemical cascades within the cell that follow receptor activation by drugs (National Institute on Drug Abuse, 1999).

These findings help us better understand the mechanisms of drug actions in the brain, but how do they help us understand the recovery process and the role of treatment? Allen Leshner, director of the National Institute on Drug Abuse, describes the task of treatment as one of dealing with the brain changes that occur in addiction; not to change the brain back, but to compensate for or reverse aspects of these brain adaptations. Behavioral as well as pharmacological methods are appropriate to accomplish these tasks. Leshner (1997) refers to studies in related fields, indicating that successful behavioral treatment of obsessive-compulsive disorders results in brain changes similar to the effect of medications.

This leads us to think of treatment in a new way. The acquisition of cognitive skills, structured social support, motivational enhancement, relapse prevention training, learning processes, and the "spiritual" experiences that may be involved in initiation and maintenance of recovery might be thought of as treatment methods to repair the brain. The mechanisms of this salutary effect of treatment need to be the focus of much additional research. Does treatment "turn on" protective genes? What kind of treatment facilitates what type of neuronal adaptations? What effects do cognitive behavioral therapy and relapse prevention techniques have on the role of dopamine and the incentive salience system as discussed in Jill Littrell's contribution to this volume?

We have evidence that treatment is effective. A considerable body of treatment services research suggests that traditional behavioral methods are effective and that the majority of clients who complete treatment do not return to dependent use of drugs (McLellan et al., 2000). We need new ways to measure this effectiveness given our new awareness of the neurochemical bases of addiction. The field needs an improved understanding of the neurobiological effects of treatment, which are associated with positive behavioral outcomes.

As a result of all this good science, what payoffs are possible to help addicted persons initiate and maintain recovery? One payoff often mentioned is the development of new medications. Another impact might be more informed genomic screening and other medical procedures for improved diagnostic and risk assessments. The possibility of gene therapy to correct or counteract genetic risk also seems to be within reach. But the greatest benefits may be in enhanced conceptual frameworks to guide treatment approaches and new technological aids such as imaging methods to measure functional or structural deficits, to evaluate behavioral methods, and to monitor treatment progress.

BARRIERS TO PROGRESS

The theme of the Summit on Social Work and the Neurobiology of Addictions was bridging the gap between neuroscience research and social work practice in the addictions. There are several dimensions of this gap. The gap between treatment services research and treatment practice was the focus of a study by the Institute of Medicine (Lamb, Greenlick, & McCarty, 1998). Health services researchers have developed an array of treatment innovations that are only partially utilized by clinicians. These include pharmacologic innovations and psychosocial methods described in Allen Zweben's paper as well as the community reinforcement approach, voucher-based reinforcement therapy, the "matrix model," node-link mapping, and improved methods of using methadone, naloxone, and other medications in combination with psychosocial methods (National Institute on Drug Abuse, 2000b). Reasons for underutilization of this treatment knowledge include financial and policy barriers as well as a lack of treatment oriented research literature and accessible technology transfer infrastructures (Lamb, Greenlick, & McCarty, 1998).

There is also a gap between services research and basic neuroscience research. More interaction is needed between these two domains to identify researchable questions to fill this void. Most neurobiological research on addictions has focused on one brain circuit at the base of the brain that runs from the ventral tegmentum to the nucleus accumbens. Little research attention has been given to the brain circuits and mechanisms involved in higher order cognitive and emotional processing that occurs in the frontal cortex as it is engaged by behavioral treatments (National Institute on Drug Abuse, 2000a). Improving treatment will require a better understanding of the cognitive factors and the corresponding brain circuits involved in addiction which must be addressed in recovery.

RESISTANCE TO CHANGE

As should be anticipated in processes involving paradigm shifts, there will be anxiety and resistance to incorporation of neurobiological constructs by some practitioners who are unfamiliar with and intimidated by the subject matter. In her article, Harriette C. Johnson identifies several other aspects of expected resistance, including fears that neurobiology may be used by those with a conservative political ideology. Some may perceive that the concept of addiction as a genetically predisposed neurological disorder precludes ability of the person to change and any meaningful role for treatment to help bring about such change. Other fears are that a neurobiological focus will negate social work's traditional emphases on socioenvironmental factors, interpersonal relationships, and psychological concepts and replace them with a mechanistic, technologically based approach, as addressed in the dialogue in this special volume between Jerry Flanzer and E. Michael Gorman. But we can also consider the positive implications this knowledge has for policy and practice. For example, knowledge of the neurobiological basis of addiction may take emphasis away from moral and deficit models and replace them with attitudes compatible with decriminalization and a greater emphasis on treatment methods to correct brain chemistry.

As change agents, the challenge we social workers face is to attend to the multiple needs of clients and the multiple concerns of addiction professionals in working through this evolution. It requires attention to the "cultural" communications gap between the sciences and the humanities (Snow, 1963). Bridging the gap between community based treatment and knowledge of the neurobiology of addictions requires active participation by practitioners and learning materials geared to the practice community of social workers and other helping professionals.

INCOMPLETE SCIENCE

Another problem of clinicians in acquiring useable neuroscientific knowledge is the evolving nature of knowledge in this area. Research advances notwithstanding, our understanding of brain processes involved in addiction is still incomplete. As illustrated in Jill Littrell's article concerning reward and motivational systems, this body of knowledge, including some of the key concepts of addiction and recovery, is still "under construction." Piecing together the findings of different researchers and sifting through partial and sometimes contradictory reports are not tasks that practitioners will happily or effectively pursue. That is why the field needs more resources for technology transfer and for the work of scientists who can provide an interpretative filter for practitioners to obtain what they need to know and can use from the broad spectrum of current scientific research. The article by Carlton K. Erickson and Richard E. Wilcox is a good illustration of how this transfer can be accomplished so that the information can be used more readily by social scientists and practitioners.

SOME FINAL CONSIDERATIONS

One final consideration for readers of this special volume is that the broader issues discussed here are not peculiar to the addictions field. Social workers need to take on the challenge of integrating neurobiological content within theoretical constructs and methods in all areas of practice. We like to describe our field as based on a biopsychosocial understanding of human functioning, yet the biological aspects are often underrepresented in our work. Harriette Johnson's contribution to this volume indicates that there are many areas of social work endeavor where neuroscience is fairly well developed and available for incorporation into curricula and practice. Efrain C. Azmitia's article on the effects of substance use and abuse throughout the life cycle provides excellent examples of this knowledge in the alcohol and drug field.

Summit participants also suggested that social workers consider more formalized ways to incorporate neurobiological knowledge in education and practice, including:

- Collaborate to develop curriculum modules for use in various social work courses.
- Request that authors and publishers include neurobiological content in human behavior texts.
- Encourage the Institute for the Advancement of Social Work Research; the Society for Social Work and Research; the Alcohol, Tobacco, and Other Drug section of NASW; and other groups to adopt action agendas to promote more research activity in this area.
- Identify and recognize investigators who make noteworthy efforts to bridge the gap between services research and basic science research.

NOTES OF APPRECIATION

We are indebted to the Waggoner Center for Alcohol and Addiction Research at the University of Texas at Austin and the Texas Commission on Alcohol and Drug Abuse (TCADA) for their financial support of the Summit and to Dr. Lala Straussner, Editor, for making this special collection possible. Thanks also to the committee of faculty and staff at the UT Austin School of Social Work that planned the summit with support from the Texas Addiction Technology Transfer Center and the UT Austin College of Pharmacy. A special thanks to all those who participated in the Summit, including faculty from 21 social work education programs across the U.S., representatives from NIDA and TCADA, and treatment providers from the Austin area.

Richard T. Spence
Diana M.DiNitto
University of Texas at Austin, School of Social Work
Texas Addiction Technology Transfer Center

REFERENCES

Lamb, S., Greenlick, M. R., & McCarty, D. (Eds.). (1998). *Bridging the gap between practice and research.* Washington D.C.: National Academy Press.

Leshner, A. I. (1997, October). Addiction is a brain disease, and it matters. *Science, 278*, 45-47.

McLellan, A. T., Lewis, D. C., O'Brien, C. P., & Kleber, H. D. (2000, October 4). Drug dependence, a chronic medical illness. *Journal of the American Medical Association, 284*, 1689-1695.

National Institute on Drug Abuse. (2000a). *Bringing the power of science to bear on drug abuse and addiction: Five year strategic plan.* (NIH Publication No. 00-4774). Rockville, MD: National Institutes of Health.

National Institute on Drug Abuse. (2000b). *Principles of drug addiction: A research-based guide.* (NIH Publication No. 00-4180). Rockville, MD: National Institutes of Health.

National Institute on Drug Abuse. (1999). *The sixth triennial report to Congress from the Secretary of Health and Human Services.* Bethesda, MD: National Institutes of Health.

Snow, C. P. (1963). *The two cultures: And a second look.* Cambridge: Cambridge University Press.

ARTICLES

Neurobiological Causes of Addiction

Carlton K. Erickson
Richard E. Wilcox

SUMMARY. Neurobiology and molecular genetics are contributing heavily to a new understanding of the causes of chemical dependence ("addiction"). Willful chemical *abuse* is a problem that continues to produce significant societal costs including accidents, medical expenses, and family suffering. Pathological chemical *dependence,* on the other hand, is being recognized as a true medical disease that is also devastating, but in different ways. There is strong evidence in animals and humans that chemical dependence involves a dysregulation of the pleasure pathway (the "medial forebrain bundle"), located in the mesolimbic portion of the brain. Dopamine is one of the medial forebrain bundle's major neurotransmitters. In this paper, we provide a research-based model for

Carlton K. Erickson, PhD, is Professor and Head, Addiction Science Research and Education Center, College of Pharmacy, The University of Texas, Austin, TX 78712 (E-mail: erickson.carl@mail.utexas.edu).

Richard E. Wilcox, PhD, is Professor, College of Pharmacy, The University of Texas, Austin, TX 78712 (E-mail: wilcoxrich@mail.utexas.edu).

[Haworth co-indexing entry note]: "Neurobiological Causes of Addiction." Erickson, Carlton K. and Richard E. Wilcox. Co-published simultaneously in *Journal of Social Work Practice in the Addictions* (The Haworth Social Work Practice Press, an imprint of The Haworth Press, Inc.) Vol. 1, No. 3, 2001, pp. 7-22; and: *Neurobiology of Addictions: Implications for Clinical Practice* (ed: Richard T. Spence, Diana M. DiNitto, and Shulamith Lala Ashenberg Straussner) The Haworth Social Work Practice Press, an imprint of The Haworth Press, Inc., 2001, pp. 7-22. Single or multiple copies of this article are available for a fee from The Haworth Document Delivery Service [1-800-342-9678, 9:00 a.m. - 5:00 p.m. (EST). E-mail address: getinfo@haworthpressinc.com].

the causes of chemical dependence and its treatment, and integrate this information with classic Twelve Step treatment programs. *[Article copies available for a fee from The Haworth Document Delivery Service: 1-800-342-9678. E-mail address: <getinfo@haworthpressinc.com> Website: <http://www.HaworthPress.com>* © *2001 by The Haworth Press, Inc. All rights reserved.]*

KEYWORDS. Drug abuse, drug dependence, medial forebrain bundle, treatment, disease, addiction, neurotransmitters

CURRENT CONTEXT OF ADDICTION RESEARCH AND TREATMENT

A significant misunderstanding has developed over the years regarding the causes of the "addictions" and what kinds of people develop addictions. Stigma, prejudice, and misunderstanding ("SPAM") cause the uninformed to believe that addicts are bad, crazy, ignorant people who only need to get good, become sane, and become educated in order to get better. SPAM is the main reason why there are insufficient funds for treatment, prevention, education, and research on addictive diseases. Therefore, it is critical that health professionals understand (a) exactly what addiction is, (b) how addictions are produced, and (c) why treatments work. Once informed, health professionals should, in turn, take a proactive role in educating the general public about the true causes and nature of dependence, as an aid to reducing SPAM and the related suffering it causes.

Terminology

The DSM-IV-TR (*Diagnostic and Statistical Manual of Mental Disorders*, Fourth Edition, Text Revision, American Psychiatric Association, 2000) provides diagnostic criteria for differentiating between "substance abuse" and "substance dependence." These are summarized in Table 1. The use of the term "substance" refers either to a chemical or to a drug. Using these criteria and other assessment tools, we can now clearly differentiate between drug *abuse,* involving a conscious choice, and drug *dependence,* in which the person has impaired control over behavior (Erickson, 1995). Thus, there are two different but related problems that must be dealt with in the so-called "drug problem" arena–abuse and dependence. Voluntary drug *abuse* is a major problem in the U.S., causing significant numbers of accidents, huge medical costs, lost productivity, and family abuse. In addition, alcohol and other drug abuse

---

TABLE 1. DSM Criteria for Drug Abuse and Dependence

Drug Abuse

A. A maladaptive pattern of drug use leading to impairment or distress, presenting as one or more of the following in a 12-month period:
 1. recurrent use leading to failure to fulfill major obligations
 2. recurrent use which is physically hazardous
 3. recurrent drug-related legal problems
 4. continued use despite social or interpersonal problems
B. The person has never met the criteria for substance dependence.

Drug Dependence

A. A maladaptive pattern of drug use, leading to impairment or distress, presenting as three or more of the following in a 12-month period:
 1. tolerance to the drug's actions
 2. withdrawal
 3. drug is used more than intended
 4. inability to control drug use
 5. effort is expended to obtain the drug
 6. important activities are replaced by drug use
 7. drug use continues in spite of negative consequences
B. Two types of dependence can occur: (a) with physiological dependence (with item 1 or 2), or (b) without physiological dependence (neither item 1 nor 2).

Adapted from Diagnostic and Statistical Manual of Mental Disorders, Fourth Edition, Text Revision, 2000.

---

usually takes its toll in terms of physical problems of the drug abuser, such as liver cirrhosis or heart problems. Abuse may be reduced by making drugs harder to get (as in reducing the number of liquor stores in a particular geographical area), punishing the individual, and by education. Drug abuse usually does not require intense intervention and treatment.

Drug *dependence,* however, is still misunderstood. Many people, including some scientists, mistakenly believe that drug-induced euphoria (well-being), craving (drug-seeking), or physical withdrawal (hyperexcitability, tremors, seizures, etc.) are causative factors in chemical dependence. Even more often, people who simply use drugs too often or in high quantities are considered to be addicted. But the DSM-IV-TR criteria (Table 1) do not include amount or frequency of use as diagnostic criteria. Furthermore, note that only the first two criteria are physiological (tolerance and withdrawal), whereas the other criteria are psychosocial. The psychosocial criteria relate to "impaired control over drug use" or the inability to stop drug use under adverse consequences. Thus, it is possible to be dependent ("addicted") without showing significant drug tolerance or dependence (seen as physical withdrawal). Conversely, people showing signs of withdrawal may not be addicted, unless they have two or more of the other criteria. This is important to point out because people often confuse withdrawal with "being addicted."

It is helpful to think of drug dependence *not* as a "too much, too often" disease, but as an "I-can't-stop" disease (Erickson, 1998). It is also useful to think of drug dependence as an "I-can't-stop" disease because it is also a "brain chemistry disease" (Leshner, 1997). In fact, it is the dysregulation of the person's brain chemistry that create the dependence, the impaired control over drug using behavior. The defining characteristic is whether a person can stop using drugs when a decision is made to stop or when a life-threatening drug-induced event occurs. This characteristic is also the one that is most often assessed through existing diagnostic methods. For example, an abuser who is faced with alcohol-induced liver cirrhosis will usually stop drinking, whereas an alcohol dependent individual (an "alcoholic") cannot stop.

Proper understanding of these definitions allows better scientific study of the true causes of pathological drug dependence (a medical disease), as compared to willful drug abuse (a social problem). These definitions also reflect what we see clinically in patients with drug difficulties.

Neurobiology of Dependence

Genetics

Many recovering addicts report that they recall vividly the first time they took a drink or used cocaine. They realized with the first drug dose that they had a special connection with the drug. Other addicts remember that they could "take it or leave it" when they were first using, but after many drug exposures they could no longer stop. This concept of "impaired control over drug use" now represents the defining characteristic of chemical dependence (addiction).

The big question in addiction science concerns how "impaired control" occurs, especially the time-course of developing dependence and its causes via changes in brain chemistry. A great deal of research on the genetics of alcohol dependence ("alcoholism") suggests that the *tendency* to become alcoholic is inherited (Cloninger, 1999). This tendency may arise as a result of altered gene functions leading to altered brain proteins. When genes are abnormal, brain enzymes and other proteins that are involved with neurotransmitter function may be abnormal. For example, the production (synthesis) or breakdown (metabolism) of dopamine is the responsibility of various enzymes. If the person has a genetic defect such that the enzymes that make or break down dopamine are faulty, then the amount of dopamine in the brain will be abnormal. Also, the response of that person's brain dopamine systems to changes in the environment may be abnormal as well. In the mesolimbic system such abnormal functions of dopamine may lead to distorted mood, such as too little pleasure from positive experiences or too much pain from negative interactions. The person with such a genetic defect may be especially susceptible to the ability of cocaine to elevate brain dopamine to levels that are closer to "normal."

Brain Chemistry

Neurotransmitters are chemical messengers in the brain. Certain potentially addictive drugs match to specific neurotransmitters. For example, cocaine matches to dopamine because its major effect is to elevate brain dopamine levels. Heroin matches the brain's natural morphine-like substances (the endorphins) because heroin mimics the effects of endorphins at their receptors. Ethanol (alcohol) is particularly troublesome because it seems to match well to several key neurotransmitters. Thus, alcohol has major effects on serotonin, GABA, glutamate, acetylcholine, dopamine, and the endorphins. Of course, nerve cells in the brain have many interconnections with other nerve cells. Thus, any brain pathway for something like pleasure will have contained in it different nerve cells that release dopamine, serotonin, endorphins, glutamate, GABA, acetylcholine, endorphins, and many more. This means that ultimately, many different addictive drugs may exert their effects through several neurotransmitter systems. For example, many scientists are proposing that there is a "final common pathway" for addictive drug effects on the mesolimbic dopamine pathway (cf. Koob et al., 1998). This pathway is also known as the medial forebrain bundle because it traverses the middle part of the base of the brain from cell bodies deep in the midbrain to innervate many structures within the frontal part of the brain (forebrain). Figure 1 illustrates these connections. What is important is that the dopamine pathway reaches a widespread portion of the brain that is concerned with emotion, pleasure, memory of emotional events, and decision-making ability for emotional events. In addition, different addictive drugs can "tap into" this dopamine pathway in several different ways. They may release dopamine, increase dopamine levels in the forebrain, or alter dopamine's actions at receptor sites. Cocaine, for example, increases mesolimbic dopamine with a single administration. Repeated cocaine exposure can lead to adaptations in the user's brain chemistry. This type of "emotional learning" represents an essentially permanent change in that person's brain wiring. Under these conditions, relative "normality" of dopamine activity and of the functions of the medial forebrain bundle are achieved only in the presence of cocaine.

Sensitization

We can reasonably assume that addicts who become dependent early in life and/or with little drug exposure are the most heavily genetically predisposed to

FIGURE 1. The Medial Forebrain Bundle

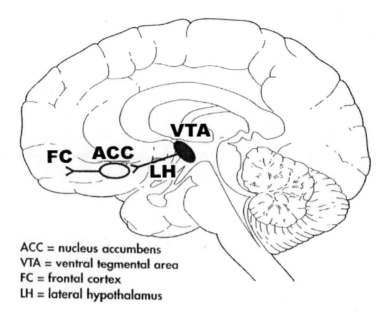

ACC = nucleus accumbens
VTA = ventral tegmental area
FC = frontal cortex
LH = lateral hypothalamus

Functional parts of the medial forebrain bundle, which is part of the mesolimbic dopamine system. The bundle consists of nerve pathways, and drug-induced activity runs from the VTA to the ACC to the FC (middle of the brain to the front of the brain). Reprinted from *Your Brain on Drugs* (1997) with permission (Hazelden, 1999).

the disease. These individuals may have more severe defects in one gene, perhaps having little ability to produce normal amounts of brain dopamine. Alternatively, these persons may have more modest genetic defects in several genes. Here, the person may produce abnormally low amounts of dopamine but also break down dopamine too efficiently. Together, this would lead to severe reductions in brain dopamine levels. For these people, a single exposure to cocaine may be life-changing because of cocaine's ability to dramatically increase levels of dopamine. This occurs because dopamine is normally removed from its receptors and "recaptured" by the releasing nerve cell through a reuptake process. Cocaine blocks this process. Thus, once dopamine is released upon nerve stimulation, its levels continue to grow in the space between nerve cells (the synaptic cleft). For people in whom genetic deficits of dopamine have led to difficulty in experiencing normal emotion, that first cocaine "high" may be the first time that they have ever had high dopamine levels ("felt normal").

Other addicts require months or years of drug use before they acquire "impaired control." It would appear that these people may have more subtle genetic defects and that a combination of factors, including exposure to the addictive agent, act in concert to activate the medial forebrain bundle. During this time, there are a variety of adaptations produced in the user's brain chemistry by the drug. For cocaine, changes in many aspects of dopamine activity can occur with repeated cocaine exposure. These include changes in transmitter production, release, interactions with receptors, return to the nerve cell, and breakdown. These changes represent the brain's attempt to adapt to the novelty of experiencing high dopamine levels. One particularly intriguing hypothesis is that nerve cells in the medial forebrain bundle that transmit the pleasurable and "craving" qualities of drugs may be "up-regulated" with chronic drug exposure. This increase in activity is termed *sensitization* (Robinson & Berridge, 1993). These pathways become more active in the drug's presence and even more active with repeated drug exposure.

However, there is a "cost" for these adaptations. The cocaine "high" is followed by a post-cocaine "low." In fact, levels of brain dopamine appear to be even lower than the person's original baseline for a period of time after the cocaine wears off. Since the cocaine "high" may be increased with repeated exposure as a result of sensitization, the cocaine "low" may also be bigger (i.e., a larger drop in dopamine occurs). While some investigators consider this to be an "acute withdrawal," it is more properly defined as an immediate rebound in which the brain attempts to return total dopamine levels over time to the original set-point for that person. Thus, drug exposure in these at-risk individuals establishes a molecular memory of the drug-taking. In particular, an enhanced (sensitized) "demand or urge" for the drug may be responsible for turning on the addictive process in these users' brains (Robinson & Berridge, 1993). Consistent with this idea, addicts often report that they "need" drugs–meaning that their body demands or requires the drug to function normally, in a manner similar to the body's need for food, water, and air. This makes sense when we understand that the medial forebrain bundle passes through the hypothalamus–a structure containing critical regulation centers such as those for eating, drinking, and breathing.

Emotional Learning

The model presented above is the "medial forebrain bundle model of impaired control" which focuses on a portion of the limbic system. Other recent work (Koob et al., 1998) has implicated the extended amygdala, a brain system that includes those areas discussed above and also the amygdala. In this view, the amygdala regulates emotional memory, and registers the significance of prior drug use. Thus, in the case of the cocaine dependent person, in addition to becoming sensitized to cocaine (having progressively larger amounts of dopamine in the areas reached by the medial forebrain bundle), the individual "learns" that cocaine fulfills a need. The extended amygdala may play either a major or an ancillary role in the production of chemical dependence. More research is necessary to clarify exactly which brain areas are involved and how they interact in the genesis and development of chemical dependence.

Non-Drug Therapies

The traditional recovery program for drug dependence is the Twelve Steps of Alcoholics Anonymous (AA). AA is a group-support process based upon principles laid out in the "Big Book" of Alcoholics Anonymous first published in the 1940s. A strong belief in, and successful "working" of the Twelve Steps, has led many people to become abstinent, and in some cases, achieve a serenity that they never previously experienced. Because of the success of the Twelve Steps, the public has developed a belief that "alcoholics and other addicts can help themselves." This is true, but not in the way that many people believe. The one decision that an addict can make is to seek help. Most people do not realize that working the Twelve Steps is a gut-wrenching, emotional, and lifetime experience that is not easy or possible for everyone to achieve. Furthermore, people in recovery and the population at large may not realize that "getting better" means that the Twelve Step process has probably changed the user's brain chemistry (Erickson, 1997).

Structured treatment systems (inpatient, outpatient, coping skills, behavioral modification) provide alternative types of help for dependent persons. Some investigators and practitioners now acknowledge the parallels between success using these approaches and using the Twelve Steps. Both types of approaches probably affect brain chemistry in a positive way. That means that a new type of learning in the emotional brain (limbic system) has occurred that can at least partially substitute for the drug-associated learning. At least part of the reason for the success of psychosocial programs lies in placing the addict in a controlled or semi-controlled environment away from the environment associated with drug taking. These programs also offer an opportunity for relearning social patterns that are helpful and provide patients with support and guidance for remaining abstinent and sober. Ancillary measures such as detoxification (when necessary), group therapy, education, exercise, meditation, and proper nutrition are designed to enhance treatment effectiveness. Each of these processes must also change the chemistry of the brain. When people get better, brain chemistry changes are postulated to occur in a direction that is positive for that individual. The chemical changes in brain chemistry that are associated with recovery restore flexibility to the individual's medial forebrain bundle and its connections. As control over the activity of dopamine and other brain chemicals is established, the person regains more control over behavior.

Relapse is a relatively common sequel to short-term treatment, and measures to prevent relapse (such as aftercare support programs and certain medications) play a major role in long-term therapy of drug dependent patients. Since treatment is usually not sought by individuals until long after the disease process has begun, it is important to understand that short-term therapy will not work for most people. One obvious way to insure long-term abstinence is to mandate long-term treatment. This gives time for substantial learning of more adaptive behaviors as a result of more substantial brain chemistry alterations due to the therapy.

Context of Drug Therapies

More recently, medications (pharmacotherapies) have become available for treatment of some types of drug dependence. It is important to remember that, at best, drug therapy can help to "reset the baseline" of that person's brain chemistry to a level closer to "normal" for that person. A single therapeutic drug cannot undue all of the negative adaptations induced by the addictive agent. On the other hand, when used in conjunction with long-term non-drug therapies (Twelve Steps, cognitive behavior therapy, etc.) the treatment period required to induce prolonged abstinence may be shortened and the likelihood of relapse reduced significantly.

Table 2 presents available medications for enhancing long-term sobriety, usually by enhancing abstinence through a reduction in craving (Wilcox & McMillen, 1998). Because craving is a subjective experience and difficult to quantify, such studies often use an objective measure–*relapse*–to assess craving. No medications currently exist that will fully normalize the brain chemistry dysfunctions that appear to drive the "need" for the drug. This is understandable given three observations discussed above. First, there are a large number of interacting transmitters (dopamine, serotonin, acetylcholine, glutamate, GABA, endorphins, etc.) that mediate reward. Second, a variety of adaptations occur to addictive drug actions, including sensitization and emotional learning. Third, the ("molecular memory") changes that occur during the development of the addiction are complex. This is because they involve several neurotransmitters and because they are time-dependent. Thus, current medications are not "magic bullets" that cure the disease. Instead, they en-

TABLE 2. Anti-Craving Medications for the Treatment of Chemical Dependencies

Dependence	Drug (Trade Name)
Cocaine	None approved, but in use: • desipramine (Norpramin) • bromocriptine (Parlodel) • amantadine (Symmetrel) • carbamazepine (Tegretol) In trial: • selegiline (Eldepryl) • disulfiram (Antabuse) • several antidepressants
Alcohol	Approved: • naltrexone (ReVia) In trial: • acamprosate • nalmefene • ondansetron (Zofran)
Heroin	Approved: • methadone (Dolophine) • L-methadyl acetate HCl (Orlaam) • naltrexone (ReVia) In trial: • buprenorphine (Buprenex)
Smoking*	Approved: • bupropion (Zyban) • nicotine patches and gum (Nicorette) • low-nicotine devices

* Technically, the medications listed for smoking cessation reduce the severity of withdrawal. It is not known whether these agents reduce craving for nicotine or smoking.

There are no FDA-approved medications for treating dependence on PCP, marijuana, methamphetamine and other stimulants, inhalants, or anabolic steroids. Vaccines for treating cocaine and nicotine dependence are currently under investigation.

hance already-established abstinence, developed through exposure to structured treatment systems or Twelve Step programs. Thus, future treatment of the addictions may usefully combine spiritually-based, psychosocial, and drug treatment with the overall aim of better living through better brain chemistry!

Drug Therapies for Detoxification

Many medications used in the treatment of drug dependence are actually used most successfully in detoxification. For example, clonidine (Catapres) and guanfacine (Tenex) are used in the treatment of heroin withdrawal. These agents are designed to make heroin withdrawal more comfortable by reducing autonomic hyperactivity that accompanies removal of the drug from the body.

Thus, both drugs mask secondary symptoms of drug withdrawal. These drugs are not a "cure" for the addiction, and they may have relatively little effect on craving. Other drugs are also used exclusively to detoxify patients and make them feel better during withdrawal. Examples are chlordiazepoxide (Librium) and diazepam (Valium) in the detoxification of alcohol dependent patients.

Drug Therapies for Reducing Relapse

Alcohol Dependence

Effective drug therapy in long-term treatment (post-withdrawal) of alcohol dependent individuals is developing quickly (Wilcox & McMillen, 1998). Two general types of agents (i.e., disulfiram and relapse-blocking drugs) are available with very different mechanisms of action. Disulfiram (Antabuse) blocks the breakdown of ethanol. This allows a toxic metabolite (acetaldehyde) to accumulate. Therefore, disulfiram induces an extremely negative (and, sometimes even lethal) consequence of ethanol consumption. Disulfiram does not affect craving. However, use of this agent may assist the person in maintaining sufficient motivation to avoid drinking until such time as non-drug therapies have induced sufficient new learning to permit the person to regain behavioral control.

Naltrexone (ReVia) blocks receptors for morphine-like substances (endorphins). It is these types of receptors that mediate the effects of heroin, related opioids, and alcohol (according to the latest speculation). Heroin normally stimulates the receptors (in the same manner that endorphins do). By blocking these receptors in alcohol dependent individuals, naltrexone prevents the effects of alcohol. When alcohol is no longer present in the body, naltrexone also keeps the individual's own endorphins from stimulating the endorphin receptors. This seems to prevent actions in the medial forebrain bundle and its neural connections that are essential for craving and relapse to occur.

Naltrexone can prevent relapse to drinking in some individuals. Naltrexone may also reduce ethanol consumption in those people who "fall off the wagon." Thus, instead of the person taking a dozen drinks, only one or two might be consumed.

Nalmefene, an experimental drug, acts very similarly to naltrexone. However, nalmefene blocks additional types of endorphin receptors beyond those blocked by naltrexone. One would predict that nalmefene should also be effective in preventing relapse in alcohol dependent people.

A potentially useful drug that is currently only available in Europe is acamprosate (calcium acetyl homotaurinate). Some investigators have suggested that acamprosate may mimic brain glutamate by stimulating some of the same receptors as glutamate. This would allow acamprosate to alter medial forebrain bundle dopamine activity indirectly. Acamprosate appears to reduce relapse to alcoholism in European clinical trials lasting 1-2 years. Controlled studies are now underway in the United States to determine if these findings can be replicated. (See Allen Zweben's article in this volume for information on related studies.)

Psychostimulants–Cocaine and Amphetamine Dependence

Antidepressant drugs and anti-Parkinson's disease agents are the types of therapeutic tools that have been most extensively investigated for possible reduction in relapse to psychostimulants. The anti-Parkinson's disease drugs fall into the category of dopamine agonists (an agonist is a drug that mimics the effect of a natural brain neurotransmitter by stimulating some of the same receptors.) Those drugs that elevate dopamine levels can do so by increasing dopamine release or by preventing dopamine reuptake into the nerve ending.

Amantadine (Symmetrel) is an anti-Parkinson's disease agent that releases dopamine. Amantadine can reduce the likelihood of relapse in at least some cocaine-dependent people. Another type of dopamine agonist is the anti-Parkinson's disease agent bromocriptine (Parlodel). Bromocriptine mimics dopamine and so can substitute for it. Bromocriptine reduces relapse to cocaine in some people. Unfortunately, bromocriptine has been abused by some at-risk individuals who consider the drug's actions to be similar to those of other addictive drugs (although more mild).

There have recently been some interesting developments in the discovery of medications to treat dependence on psychostimulant drugs. First, one of the newer drugs is GVG (gamma-vinyl-GABA, Sabril). GVG blocks the breakdown of GABA. A reduced breakdown means increased levels of GABA in the brain. GVG seems able to inhibit the increases in dopamine in some of the terminal areas of the medial forebrain bundle that are typically produced by administration of ethanol, heroin, or methamphetamine. GVG is one of about a dozen new anti-epilepsy drugs that might also be of at least some benefit in treating drug dependent people. Clinical studies are ongoing.

Second, a vaccine has been made that blocks cocaine's effects in animals. This vaccine reduces the amount of cocaine reaching the brain and prevents at least some of the increase in dopamine that cocaine would normally produce. It is now in clinical trials to determine whether it can be effective in blocking the addictive effects of cocaine or the problems with cocaine overdose in humans.

One of the major problems with medications development, especially for cocaine dependence, is demonstrating that the medications produce more than the usual positive placebo effect seen in most controlled clinical trials.

Heroin Dependence

In the brain, heroin is converted to morphine so that the effects are actually those of morphine. Methadone is the mainstay of current treatment for heroin dependence. Methadone and heroin are both direct agonists at the brain's receptors for morphine (endorphins). Thus, heroin and methadone (and morphine) mimic the endorphins. This means that methadone binds to the same receptors as heroin, activates the same receptors as heroin, and induces the same effects inside nerve cells as heroin. Another agonist, LAAM (L-alpha-acetyl-methadol), acts in the same manner as methadone but has a longer action. LAAM and methadone both prevent relapse in heroin dependent individuals because they substitute for heroin and thus reduce the craving for heroin.

There are a number of drugs that block endorphin receptors and, thereby, prevent heroin from activating the receptors. This means that such blocking drugs can induce withdrawal in someone dependent on heroin when heroin is still present in the body. The short-acting blocker, naloxone (Narcan) and the longer acting drug naltrexone (ReVia, formerly Trexan) have both been used in heroin detoxification because of their ability to displace heroin from its active sites in the brain. Even after the heroin is eliminated from an individual's body, both naloxone and naltrexone may still be useful because these blocking drugs reduce relapse by reducing the heroin craving. There is now even a very long-acting ("depot") form of naltrexone that allows naltrexone delivery for up to 30 days. Because naltrexone can prevent heroin from having an effect, the dependent person knows that money would be wasted trying to get "high" from heroin.

Whereas a *full agonist* is a drug that produces as much of an effect inside a nerve cell as the natural neurotransmitter, a *partial agonist* is a drug that produces a smaller effect. Buprenorphine (Buprenex) is a partial agonist at the brain's endorphin receptors. What this means is that, even though buprenorphine attaches to (binds to) the endorphin receptors as well as heroin, methadone, LAAM, or morphine, buprenorphine is less able to mimic the effects of these drugs inside the nerve cell. This gives buprenorphine and drugs with similar mechanisms of action a potentially unique capability. They act enough like the addictive drug to prevent withdrawal (partially substituting for the addicting drug) but enough like a blocking drug that they may reduce the likelihood of relapse.

Nicotine Dependence

A cigarette has been described (by executives of the tobacco industry) as the perfect delivery system for nicotine. Basically, there are two different ways that people dependent on nicotine can prevent relapse to smoking. First, they can try a form of substitution therapy (similar to using methadone for heroin or methylphenidate for cocaine). In this case the person takes in the nicotine in a different form than smoking. Thus, nicotine patches or nicotine gum are among the more popular delivery systems. Three beneficial things happen with their use. First, the nicotine dependent person gets the nicotine but with a less extreme nicotine high than provided by smoking. Second, the person avoids inhaling carcinogens contained in tobacco smoke. The nicotine dependent person still gets the nicotine craving but now uses the drug in a somewhat safer form (although nicotine itself is toxic to the heart). Third, nicotine substitution therapy provides the motivated smoker with a means to gradually taper the nicotine levels to complete abstinence.

The second form of drug therapy for smokers involves a particular antidepressant drug, bupropion (Zyban). Bupropion acts by a mechanism that is different from nicotine substitution. Bupropion seems to increase the amount of dopamine in the brain. Nicotine does this as well. Thus, bupropion appears to reduce nicotine craving by providing a "partial substitution" for one of nicotine's major actions. In addition, bupropion reduces the depression associated with the cessation of smoking that may be part of the nicotine withdrawal syndrome.

Watch for a new nicotine vaccine, now under development in animals. This vaccine, like that of the cocaine vaccine, is designed to prevent nicotine from reaching its receptor sites in the brain.

CONCLUSIONS

Many drug dependent individuals may be more effectively treated if they are given drugs as adjuncts to other types of therapy (Twelve Steps, psychosocial, etc.). For many individuals, we speculate that the drug therapy and the non-drug therapy should be of long-term duration. Most of the pharmacotherapy studies have been relatively short term. We don't really know how long each type of therapy must be continued to maintain lifetime abstinence.

A fundamental tenet of modern medicine is that a holistic approach is more effective than any single type of therapy. Even more than with psychiatric illnesses such as bipolar disorder and schizophrenia, treatment of the addictions represents an excellent example of a true holistic approach to patient care in medicine. All members of a modern health care team (social worker, pharmacist, physician, nurse, and the patient) have valuable contributions to make in managing the long-term treatment of an individual's dependence. Each can contribute information and approaches that will assist a drug dependent person in establishing new methods of dealing with the addiction. Combining these highly sophisticated and adaptive changes in brain chemistry induced by traditional therapies with drugs that are better targeted to reset brain chemistry baselines in the addicted person is a goal that is within reach.

Classic medical diseases including Parkinson's disease, schizophrenia, heart disease, diabetes, and tuberculosis share many significant similarities with the addictions. Each classic disease and the addictions cause changes in body chemistry. All of these diseases show a good clinical response to specific therapeutic drugs. Drugs for all of these disorders typically need to be given over the person's lifetime. The afflicted person does not have conscious control over the onset of the disease, although in many cases (for example, heart disease and diabetes) the person's choices directly lead to the symptoms. Both the classic and addictive diseases are long-term and progressive without "perfect" therapies and cures. For all of the diseases, the sooner treatment is initiated, the better the result for the patient. Finally, every single one of these diseases (including the addictions) will eventually kill the patient or destroy the quality of life. It is for all of these reasons that the newest research is exciting and important in attacking dependence on drugs, one of the leading public health problems in the world.

REFERENCES

American Psychiatric Association (2000). *Diagnostic and Statistical Manual of Mental Disorders*, Fourth Edition, Text Revision. Washington, D.C.: American Psychiatric Association.

Cloninger, C. R. (1999). *Textbook of Substance Abuse Treatment*. Washington, D.C.: American Psychiatric Press, Inc.

Erickson, C. K. (1995). Voice of the victims: There is a difference between alcohol abuse and alcoholism. *Alcoholism: Clinical and Experimental Research*, *19*, 533-534.

Erickson, C. K. (1997). Voices of the afflicted: How does alcoholism treatment work? A neurochemical hypothesis. *Alcoholism: Clinical and Experimental Research*, *21*, 567-568.

Erickson, C. K. (1998). Voices of the afflicted: What is impaired control? *Alcoholism: Clinical and Experimental Research*, *22*, 132-133.

Koob, G. F., Sanna, P. P., & Bloom, F. E. (1998). Neuroscience of addiction. *Neuron*, *21*, 467-476.

Leshner, A. I. (1997). Addiction is a brain disease. *Science*, *278*, 45-47.

Robinson, T. E. & Berridge, K. C. (1993). The neural basis of drug craving: An incentive-sensitization theory of addiction. *Brain Research Reviews*, *18*, 246-291.

Wilcox, R. E. & McMillen, B. A. (1998). The rational use of drugs as therapeutic agents for the treatment of the alcoholisms. *Alcohol*, *15*, 161-177.

What Neurobiology Has to Say
About Why People Abuse Alcohol
and Other Drugs

Jill Littrell

SUMMARY. Four major hypotheses have been formulated to address the issue of why some people develop compulsive use of particular drugs. These hypotheses include: (1) Drugs that are abused sensitize the motivational systems of the brain such that the behavioral routines for acquisition of the drug become compulsive, (2) Drugs that are abused stimulate the pleasure centers in the brain, (3) People who abuse drugs are naturally in an aversive state that their drug use enables them to escape, and (4) Drugs of abuse are associated with aversive withdrawal phenomena which can be elicited by conditioned stimuli, therefore people continue to take drugs to avert conditioned withdrawal states. This paper examines each of these hypotheses in light of research findings from neurobiology. *[Article copies available for a fee from The Haworth Document Delivery Service: 1-800-342-9678. E-mail address: <getinfo@haworthpressinc.com> Website: <http://www.HaworthPress.com> © 2001 by The Haworth Press, Inc. All rights reserved.]*

KEYWORDS. Neurobiology, addiction, nucleus accumbens, motivation, drug use

Jill Littrell, PhD, is Associate Professor of Social Work, Georgia State University, 585 Indian Acres Court, Tucker, GA 30084 (E-mail: littrell@gsu.edu).

[Haworth co-indexing entry note]: "What Neurobiology Has to Say About Why People Abuse Alcohol and Other Drugs." Littrell, Jill. Co-published simultaneously in *Journal of Social Work Practice in the Addictions* (The Haworth Social Work Practice Press, an imprint of The Haworth Press, Inc.) Vol. 1, No. 3, 2001, pp. 23-40; and: *Neurobiology of Addictions: Implications for Clinical Practice* (ed: Richard T. Spence, Diana M. DiNitto, and Shulamith Lala Ashenberg Straussner) The Haworth Social Work Practice Press, an imprint of The Haworth Press, Inc., 2001, pp. 23-40. Single or multiple copies of this article are available for a fee from The Haworth Document Delivery Service [1-800-342-9678, 9:00 a.m. - 5:00 p.m. (EST). E-mail address: getinfo@haworthpressinc.com].

INTRODUCTION

A basic question for clinicians who treat substance abusers and for practitioners dedicated to the prevention of substance abuse is "Why do particular people develop compulsive use of some chemicals?" This paper evaluates, in light of recent neurobiological findings, four hypotheses that have been advanced in the literature addressing this question. The focus then shifts to implications for primary prevention and relapse prevention of substance abuse.

Hypothesis 1: Chemicals that activate the brain's incentive-salience system are likely to trigger compulsive use of these chemicals.

The discovery of the brain's incentive-salience system began with a reflection upon two previously researched phenomena: kindling and sensitization. This section begins with an explanation of these phenomena.

Kindling and Sensitization

Neurobiologists have long been aware of a phenomenon referred to as kindling. Kindling describes a process wherein animals exposed to a small amount of electrical stimulation in the amygdala, insufficient to produce a seizure, will eventually lower the threshold for eliciting a seizure. That is, animals with prior exposure to electrical stimulation in the brain need less electrical stimulation to trigger a seizure than do animals that have not been previously stimulated with electricity (Post & Weiss, 1988).

Neurobiologists then noticed another phenomenon that they thought might reflect the same process as observed in kindling. Namely, animals exposed over time to stimulant drugs (amphetamine, Ritalin or methylphenidate, cocaine, bromocriptine, apomorphine) needed lesser amounts of these drugs to trigger certain behaviors. These behaviors included locomotion or motoric activity, and stereotypy (highly stereotyped, narrowly focused, repetitive behaviors). Later, researchers recognized that these behaviors probably reflected dopamine release in particular brain structures (viz. ventral tegmental area, the nucleus accumbens, and the basal ganglia). Additionally, given repeated exposure to stimulant drugs over time, the amount of dopamine released in these structures increased in response to a standard dose of a stimulant drug. The animals were seemingly "sensitized" to the stimulant drugs (Robinson & Berridge, 1993).

Another behavioral manifestation of the sensitization process was noticed as well. Animals seemed to work harder for a stimulant drug. Moreover, the behavior of working for stimulant drugs became increasingly resistant to extinction. Over time, the drugs seemed to become increasingly more attractive (Robinson & Berridge, 1993).

Then it was discovered that not only stimulant drugs, but other events could sensitize the release of dopamine in relevant structures. Stressful conditions, hunger, opioids, and the stress hormone CRF (corticotropin releasing factor) could also sensitize the system. An animal exposed to stressful conditions (restraint stress, tail shock, etc.) needed less cocaine to elicit dopamine release, locomotion, more robust lever pressing for the cocaine, and stereotypy. Moreover, an animal that had been given low doses of Ritalin required lesser exposure to stressful conditions in order to elicit dopamine release and behaviors such as locomotion and stereotypy. Cross-sensitization among the various conditions that could induce sensitization seemed to apply (Robinson & Berridge, 1993; Robinson, 1988).

It was later recognized that contextual stimuli associated with the administration of stimulant drugs or stressors also were able to elicit neurotransmitter release, locomotion, and stereotypy. Moreover, part of the capacity of repeated drug exposure to elicit these reactions was due not to the drug itself but rather to the conditioned stimuli associated with the administration of the stimulant drug. This is seen, for example, when animals stimulated by a drug in one environment are re-stimulated with the drug in a different environment. In these cases, the amount of dopamine released, the degree of locomotion manifested, and the degree of stereotypy manifested were similar to the levels exhibited by an animal never exposed to stimulants (Robinson & Berridge, 1993).

Researchers also questioned whether particular animals were more susceptible to sensitization with stimulant drugs. They discovered that animals that are more behaviorally active in novel situations were more susceptible to the stimulant sensitization (Robinson & Berridge, 1993).

Of course, neurobiologists not only want to know the conditions that will elicit a phenomenon, they also want to know how to block a phenomenon. Not surprisingly, a host of dopaminergic antagonists (Haldol, Pimozide) blocked an animal's initial response to a stimulant, as well as blocking the process of sensitization (Robinson & Berridge, 1993). Naloxone, an opioid antagonist, also blocked sensitization (Stewart & Vezina, 1988). Animals whose dopamine neuron tracts had been destroyed could not be sensitized (Robinson & Berridge, 1993).

The Incentive-Salience System

Simultaneously with the exploration of how animals respond to drugs, other scientists were asking questions about the nature of reinforcement and the neurobiological underpinnings of love and basic reinforcers such as food and sex. Killeen (1975) and Killeen, Hanson, and Osborn (1978), who explored the effects of operant conditioning, showed that the initial response of an animal to the administration of a reinforcer was increased activity or locomotion. The presentation of stimuli that had been previously associated with the administration of a reinforcer also resulted in enhanced activity or locomotion.

Investigators were trying to identify specific brain structures and neurotransmitter systems associated with reward. Researchers found that dopaminergic neurons fire upon the presentation of stimuli signaling the availability of natural reinforcers, such as food and sex; during activity directed toward obtaining a reward; and during the performance of active avoidance behavior. As the reward is consumed, dopaminergic activity subsides. The amount of dopamine released correlates with the locomotion observed when the animals are presented with a stimulus indicating that rewards are available (Berridge & Robinson, 1998).

Neurobiologists are accustomed to ablating (destroying) whole tracts of neurons and observing the effect on behavior. After the dopaminergic tracts were destroyed in the mesolimbic and nigro-striatal pathways, the animal would not eat or drink water. Even though the animals could move, they would not exhibit behavior directed toward obtaining food or water (Berridge & Robinson, 1998; Salamone, Zigmond, & Stricker, 1990). Moreover, if animals were given a dopamine antagonist that would suppress neuronal activity in the mesolimbic and nigrostriatal pathways, the animal would no longer exert effort to obtain a previously preferred food, although it would continue to eat bland food for which it did not have to work (Berridge & Robinson, 1998).

Curiously, these dopaminergic tract deficient animals still could enjoy food. Activity in brain structures associated with consumption of sucrose, a preferred food, was apparent when the animal was force-fed sucrose. There was further evidence that dopaminergic destruction did not alter an animal's emotional reactions of enjoyment of or repulsion from particular foods. LiCl, a substance which if paired with sucrose rendered sucrose aversive as evidence by a gagging response, still operated to condition sucrose aversion in a dopamine-tract deficient animal. A dopamine-tract deficient animal could still display the normal facial gestures in response to sucrose (licking the preferred food) and to quinine (gagging when swallowing this aversive liquid). Drugs that enhanced an animal's positive response to foods, such as opioids and benzodiazepines, still enhanced licking when a dopamine-deficient animal was forced to ingest sucrose. Thus, an animal whose dopamine tracts had been destroyed was still capable of "liking things" although the capacity to "want things" (expend effort toward a goal) had been eliminated (Berridge & Robinson, 1998).

These observations regarding the function of dopaminergic tracts in the processes of reinforcement and sensitization have led Berridge and Robinson

(1998) and Robinson and Berridge (1993) to conclude that dopaminergic systems can best be regarded as the "incentive-salience" system. When activated, these structures result in behavior and cravings that direct an animal toward reward acquisition. These structures are the basis for "wanting."

Beyond its role in inducing an animal to engage in goal directed activity, the "incentive-salience" system also plays a role in enhancing an animal's capacity to learn new associations. When the incentive-salience system is activated, an animal more readily acquires information about the significance of new cues signaling the availability of reward. That is, it becomes easier to develop associations between new conditioned stimuli and a reinforcer, and it is harder to extinguish responses to previously conditioned stimuli. Latent inhibition, the phenomenon wherein a stimulus with which the animal is very familiar cannot acquire new positive or negative associations, is more easily overcome. Conditioned stimuli for a broad range of reinforcers (sex and food) have a stronger directing effect on the animal's behavior (Berridge & Robinson, 1998; Robinson & Berridge, 1993).

In addition, to the effects on learning, Salamone (1992; Salamone, Aberman, Sokolowski, & Cousins, 1999) has highlighted the energizing effects of the incentive-salience system. When structures of the incentive-salience system are activated, the response costs of working toward a goal are lowered. The animal is willing to expend more effort.

Drugs associated with compulsive use (cocaine, amphetamine, Ritalin, opioids, ethanol) all share a capacity for activating dopamine release in the brain structures associated with incentive-salience (ventral tegmental area, nucleus accumbens, ventral palladium). Stimuli associated with compulsive-drug use can also activate the dopamine activity in incentive-salience associated structures (Berridge & Robinson, 1998). Thus, strong activation of incentive-salience structures can be elicited by conditioned stimuli associated with drug use. This latter finding seemed to explain Childress et al.'s (1999) finding that cocaine-use-associated-paraphernalia can elicit craving and enhanced activity in the amygdala and the cingulate gyrus, regions connected with the nucleus accumbens. Moreover, craving is associated with elevated plasma and cerebrospinal-fluid levels of HVA (a dopamine metabolite) consistent with activation of the incentive-salience structures (Robinson & Berridge, 1993).

In summary, neurobiological research led to the discovery of brain structures (the incentive-salience system) that are active during a subjective state of compulsion and during the performance of vigorous goal directed activity. Surprisingly, activity in these structures is not always associated with the subjective experience of pleasure. The discovery of the incentive-salience system, along with the elucidation of its operation, provided an unexpected answer to the question, "Why do people take drugs?" When the incentive-salience system is activated by a drug, the motivation system is captured. For the hapless individual, his/her drug acquisition behavior will be compelled by the brain's incentive-salience system, even when this behavior makes no sense to other parts of the brain (the cortex), does not feel volitional, and may not result in any subjective pleasure. Understanding the operation of the incentive-salience system provides a scientific explanation for the "loss of control" phenomenon.

Hypothesis 2: Drugs that lead to compulsive use do so because of their capacity to induce pleasure or enjoyment.

In 1987, Wise and Bozarth observed that all the drugs that lead to compulsive use share a capacity for inducing dopamine release in the ventral tegmental area of the brain which projects to the prefrontal cortex, the nucleus accumbens, the ventral palladium, and other structures. Moreover, all of these compulsive use-inducing substances satisfy the definition of a reinforcer, since animals will work for their administration and these drugs can be used to induce conditioned place preference, i.e., animals will prefer to spend time in locations where they previously received these drugs. Although behaviorists had long cautioned against the inference that reinforcers are necessarily associated with enjoyment, it was easy to leap to the conclusion that a substance for which animals will work, or which induce conditioned place preference, are enjoyed. Additionally, some concluded that since drugs that lead to compulsive use also increase dopamine activity, and because dopaminergic tracts overlap with brain areas for electrical self-stimulation, dopamine is the brain's pleasure neurotransmitter, i.e., dopamine is the brain's pleasure neurotransmitter (Wise & Rompre, 1989).

Later, evidence emerged that challenged the notion that dopamine mediated pleasure. Findings arguing against the conclusion that dopamine activity and dopaminergic tracts are the "pleasure system" included:

1. Aversive events (tail shock, hunger, restraint), anxiogenic drugs, and performance of active avoidance are also associated with activity in dopamine neurons and enhanced dopamine release in the nucleus accumbens.

2. Animals whose dopamine neurons have been destroyed are still able to exhibit behaviors associated with consumption of preferred foods (i.e., licking) and behaviors associated with food aversion (i.e., gagging). That is, they continue to manifest affect.

3. Dopamine release is most evident when an animal works for a reward, but decreases when an animal consumes or receives a reward. Assuming that pleasure should be greater when consuming a reward than when working for it, this finding further contradicted the "dopamine equals pleasure" hypothesis.

In view of the foregoing data, many researchers have concluded that dopamine tracts cannot be viewed as the neurotransmitter mediating the subjective experience of pleasure (Berridge & Robinson, 1998; Rada, Mark, & Hoebel, 1998; Salamone, Cousins, & Snyder, 1997; Wise & Rompre, 1989).

Of course, rejecting the "dopamine activation equals pleasure" hypothesis comports well with the "incentive-salience" theory. Unfortunately, a critical experiment for the theory of incentive-salience has not yet been conducted. Researchers have not yet destroyed structures associated with "liking" to determine if an animal still retains the capacity to sensitize the incentive-salience system and/or to develop a compulsive pattern of drug use. Although some of the brain structures undergirding pleasure (opioid tracts in the shell of the nucleus accumbens, particular nuclei in the ventral palladium, opioid tracks in the forebrain, etc.) have been identified, it is unclear whether these structures mediate all forms of pleasure or, rather, are specific to only certain types of pleasure (Berridge & Robinson, 1998). Indeed, Berridge (1999) indicates that brain structures underpinning pleasure are probably more diffuse as would be expected of a response that is less closely associated with specific stimuli. Without the identification of all pleasure circuits, it is impossible to determine whether their input to the incentive-salience system is required for the development of compulsion. Thus, it is unknown whether brain structures undergirding pleasure are necessary for the development of compulsive, goal-directed behavior. What is clear is that the activation of these pleasure structures alone, without the dopaminergic circuitry, is not sufficient for the development of compulsive behavior (Berridge & Robinson, 1998).

In a study by Lamb et al. (1991), human subjects who had been dependent on opioids (but who were not at the time in a withdrawal state) worked for infusions of either morphine or a placebo. Lamb et al. found that at high dosage levels of morphine, addicts identified the unlabeled infusions as pleasurable and worked for these infusions. However, they also worked for low dose infusion of morphine even though the addicts could not distinguish the active infusion from the placebo and did not label the infusion as pleasurable. In contrast, they did not work for placebo infusions. Perhaps low morphine dosages were sufficient to engage the addict's incentive-salience system manifesting in work for their drug, although the dosage level was not sufficient to induce a subjective experience of pleasure. The Lamb et al. study may imply that subjective pleasure is not necessary for compulsion. However, it is also possible that the pleasure circuitry was stimulated by the low dosage of morphine but that the activation was below the threshold for awareness.

What can be concluded here? We know that drugs associated with compulsive use activate dopamine release in incentive-salience structures. However, dopamine release is not synonymous with pleasure. Activation of dopamine associated structures is critical for the development of compulsive use of stimulant drugs. Thus, although some compulsion-inducing drugs may indeed induce a state of pleasure, this induction of pleasure does not induce compulsive drug use.

Hypothesis 3: Individuals develop compulsive drug use because it enables them to escape their natural dysphoric state.

This hypothesis contains two premises: Compulsion-inducing drugs can induce a subjective state of pleasure that can eclipse negative feelings, and individuals who are at risk for addiction are in a natural state of dysphoria that they wish to escape. Since the issue of whether compulsion-inducing drugs are associated with pleasure was discussed earlier, this section will focus on individual risk factors for addiction and related research which fails to support these two premises.

Identifying genes and personality traits associated with genetic factors that may predispose individuals to drug dependence has been an area of vigorous research. Sensation-seeking, a correlate of extraversion (Ball & Zuckerman, 1992), has been consistently identified as a predisposing factor. A few relevant findings can be cited to bolster this case. Sensation-seeking correlates with particular alleles (variants of particular genes) for the dopamine receptor gene which are, in turn, associated with difficulty in smoking cessation (Sabol et al., 1999). Sensation-seeking in young persons is a predictor of future cigarette use (Lipkus, Barefoot, Williams, & Siegler, 1994). Sensation-seeking is more prevalent in children of alcoholics than in the general population, and the effect of FHP (family-history-positive) status on greater alcohol consumption is mediated through sensation seeking (Finn, Sharkansky, Brandt, & Turcotte, 2000). Sensation seeking is also higher among substance using adolescents (Donohew et al., 1999) and sensation-seeking and attention-deficit/hyperactivity disorder (ADHD) predict future drug dependence (Disney, Elkins, McGure, & Iacono, 1999; Sabol et al., 1999). Having a family history for alcoholism and extraversion predicts an earlier age of onset for drinking. Statistical analysis shows that the effect of family history on early onset drinking is mediated through extraversion (Hill & Yuan, 1999). Extraversion is a predictor of alcohol dependence in young adults (Kilbey, Downey, & Breslau, 1998).

Findings in the literature on humans are consistent with animal research. Rodents that are most susceptible to sensitization of dopamine structures when given a stimulant are more reactive to novelty (Hooks, Jones, Neill, & Justice, 1992; Hooks, Jones, Smith, Neill, & Justice, 1991; Robinson & Berridge, 1993). Rat strains that display enhanced preference for alcohol are naturally more active, display more activity in response to alcohol consumption, and are less prone to sedation by alcohol (Li, 2000; Li et al., 1989). Thus, genetically based behaviors such as sensation-seeking, novelty-seeking, and/or high-activity level appear to be risk factors for addictive drug use in both humans and animals.

If the hypothesis that particular individuals develop compulsive use of drugs because they are seeking to escape a naturally aversive condition is correct, then the personality-risk factors for compulsive drug use should be associated with dysphoria. In fact, the reverse is true. Extraversion correlates positively with positive affect (Watson, Clark, McIntyre, & Hamaker, 1992). Given stressful conditions, sensation-seekers are less likely to exhibit dysphoria than are other persons (Smith, Ptacek, & Smoll, 1992). Moreover, rat strains that prefer alcohol are less susceptible to the effects of stress as measured by the defensive burying test and ulcer development (Sandbak, Murison, Sarviharju, & Hyytia, 1998). Thus, the genetic predisposition to drug use does not seem to involve emotional pain or susceptibility to dysphoria.

The fact that some individuals develop a compulsive drug use pattern in response to emotional pain cannot be denied. In the case of alcoholism, about 5-10% of those who are alcohol dependent can be labeled as having primary depression with secondary alcoholism. For these individuals, depression preceded their alcoholism. It is likely that these individuals began using alcohol to attenuate their negative moods. However, they are less likely to have a family history of alcoholism than primary alcoholics (Littrell, 1991a), and, thus, their alcoholism is less likely to be genetically based. Additionally, women, for whom the case for inherited alcoholism is less well established, are more likely to display this form of alcoholism (Littrell, 1991a; 1991b). In contrast, about 85% of alcoholics are high scorers on the MacAndrew scale, an MMPI scale whose items overlap with items on the Sensation Seeking Scale (Littrell, 1991a). They are more likely to be primary alcoholics for whom depression was not apparent prior to the inception of their drinking careers (Littrell, 1991a). Moving beyond alcohol to other drugs, sensation seeking is probably the strongest trait predictor of compulsive drug use (Sabol et al., 1999). Therefore, it is unlikely that primary alcoholics and sensation-seeking individuals began their drug use careers in order to medicate depression, because, as a group, they are less likely to be depressed.

Hypothesis 4: Drug use is an attempt to escape from an aversive state of conditioned withdrawal.

Drugs leading to compulsive use patterns are associated with withdrawal symptoms upon discontinuation of the drug. Alcohol withdrawal consists of dysphoria, seizures, tremulousness, impaired cognition, elevated blood pressure, and nausea, among other symptoms (Littrell, 1991b). Nicotine abstinence syndrome consists of irritability, impaired concentration, restlessness, depression, and sleep disturbance (American Psychiatric Association, 1996). Cocaine and amphetamine withdrawal is associated with fatigue, irritability, depression, and lethargy (Extein & Dackis, 1987). Finally, opiate withdrawal is associated with muscle soreness, insomnia, anxiety, enhanced sexual responsivity, and diarrhea (Grilly, 1998). It is well documented that contextual stimuli associated with the environment in which withdrawal from a substance occurred can come to elicit withdrawal phenomenon in a long abstinent individual (Robinson & Berridge, 1993). Animals will also work to escape withdrawal symptoms (Schulteis & Koob, 1996).

Wikler (1973) advanced the hypothesis that, because alcoholics had so frequently experienced withdrawal symptoms, many stimuli had become conditioned stimuli with the capacity for eliciting a conditioned withdrawal state. Wikler reasoned that since drug use can quell withdrawal symptoms, therein allowing escape from an aversive state, individuals learn to escape conditioned withdrawal through drug use. Thus, states of conditioned withdrawal might motivate relapse after a period of abstinence. Similar arguments have been proffered with regard to other drugs (Piasecki et al., 2000).

However, an early finding casts doubt on this hypothesis. Tamerin, Weiner, and Mendelson (1970) observed alcoholics drinking under varied environmental conditions. These researchers offered alcoholics, in the midst of withdrawal, the option of either using their token earnings to obtain a small amount of alcohol to avert withdrawal, or saving up their tokens for a large quantity of alcohol to be consumed some time in the future. More subjects chose to reserve their tokens for the larger amount of alcohol than to escape their withdrawal.

Additional data argued against the "escape from aversive withdrawal" as a crucial motivation for compulsive drug use. Phenothiazines (e.g., Haldol, Thorazine) and anticholinergics (e.g., Benadryl) are associated with unpleasant withdrawal phenomenon; yet these drugs do not lead to compulsive use (Robinson & Berridge, 1993). Chemicals which suppress withdrawal symptoms (e.g., low dosage nicotine patch) do not decrease the probability of relapse (Jorenby et al., 1995; Piasecki et al., 2000). Withdrawal severity and reports of craving are not correlated (Robinson & Berridge, 1993). Drug priming induces stronger craving than does withdrawal (Robinson & Berridge, 1993).

Findings from human studies are mirrored in animal research. Inducing withdrawal in opiate-addicted animals does not induce drug seeking. Although during withdrawal, footshock stress increases drug seeking (Shaham, Rajabi, & Stewart, 1996).

Returning to the idea of the incentive-salience structures (which include the nucleus accumbens and ventral tegmental area), there are additional reasons why withdrawal states do not explain drug compulsions. During withdrawal from cocaine, opiates, and alcohol, release of dopamine in the nucleus accumbens is suppressed. The symptoms of withdrawal include a higher threshold for brain self-stimulation, diminished operant responding for food, and diminished spontaneous locomotion (Schulteis & Koob, 1996). If craving and working for drugs are mediated by robust dopamine release in the nucleus accumbens (Knoblich et al., 1992), withdrawal states probably preclude this release and associated enthusiastic activity.

Thus, although there is no doubt that drugs associated with compulsive use are also associated with aversive withdrawal symptoms, it is unlikely that escape from these withdrawal symptoms accounts for drug compulsion. However, there is no question that individuals may occasionally seek escape from this unpleasant condition.

IMPLICATIONS OF THE NEUROBIOLOGICAL FINDINGS

Primary Prevention of Drug Addiction

Neurobiological research alerts us to those most at risk for drug abuse. Animals prone to novelty seeking are more susceptible to sensitization of their dopaminergic tracts by stimulant drugs (Robinson & Berridge, 1993). This finding is consistent with the larger literature emerging on genetic susceptibility to drug addiction in humans. Sensation-seeking and ADHD predispose individuals to drug dependence (Disney et al., 1999; Littrell, 1991b; Sabol et al., 1999). Certainly these individuals should be targeted by our prevention programs.

In addition, the literature on cross-sensitization identifies events in a person's life that could also increase the likelihood of development of a compulsive drug use pattern. These conditions include exposure to chemicals such as Ritalin and alcohol, and exposure to stressful conditions. Again, this knowledge should help to identify persons toward whom prevention programs should be directed.

Relapse Prevention

The literature on the incentive-salience system identifies conditions that will activate the system and stimulate drug seeking behavior and craving: exposure to stressors, food deprivation, priming doses of stimulant drugs or alcohol, and exposure to cues associated with prior drug use (Robinson & Berridge, 1993). Many of these relapse precipitants have long been recognized by Alcoholics Anonymous members who advise against being "hungry, angry, lonely, tired," and frequenting "slippery places," as well as enjoining any use of psychoactive chemicals. Much of the relapse-precipitant therapy focuses on identifying environmental cues which might initiate craving. Behaviorists have advised supervised exposure to conditioned cues associated with drug use (e.g., drug paraphernalia) to promote relearning (extinction) (Bouton, 2000). Moreover, informing clients that drug use may increase cravings (Robbins & Ehrman, 1998) may assist in motivating abstinence.

There are, however, some puzzling findings in the literature. Craving during treatment is not a good predictor of alcohol relapse following treatment (Flannery, Volpicelli, & Pettinati, 1999). Ritalin treatment of the formerly cocaine dependent with ADHD reduces cocaine relapse (Levin, Evans, McDowell, & Kleber, 1998). If compulsive use is explained by a person's dispositional characteristics and the impact of chemicals, these findings are inconsistent with theory. Perhaps they can be explained by additional findings that qualify incentive-salience theory. Stimulant drugs will fail to activate the incentive-salience system (priming craving and drug seeking) if the stimulant drug is presented in a context different from that in which the incentive-salience system was originally sensitized (Stewart & Vezina, 1988). Moreover, conditioned stimuli associated with particular sensory modalities (gustatory or olfactory) elicit differing conditioned responses, even though they have been paired with the same unconditioned stimulus, viz. morphine (Bevins & Bardo, 1998). Thus, consideration must be given as to which contextual cues associated with initial drug use will activate the incentive-salience system for the particular individual. Indeed cravings may never occur if the *relevant* contextual cues are avoided (Wise, 1999). Because the relevant contextual cues for eliciting cravings may not be immediately obvious, part of the treatment process should be devoted to identifying those particular cues that might serve as a relapse precipitant for a particular client.

Adjunctive Drugs for Preventing Relapse

The federal government has invested heavily in developing and identifying chemicals that might prevent relapse in former drug addicts. In our enthusiasm to decrease relapse, it is important to remember that any drug which operates on the incentive-salience system probably will have an influence on all basic processes involving goal-directed behavior.

Many outcome studies have examined the impact of Naloxone on attenuating relapse to alcohol abuse (O'Malley, Croop, Wroblewski, Labriola, & Volpicelli, 1995; O'Malley et al., 1992; Volpicelli, Alterman, Hayashida, & O'Brien, 1992), opiate use (Osborn, Grey, & Reznikoff, 1986), and cocaine use (Kosten et al., 1992; Walsh, Sullivan, Preston, Garner, & Bieglow, 1996). Dependent variables in these studies have included time to relapse, number of relapses (Jaffe et al., 1996; O'Malley et al., 1992; Volpicelli et al., 1997), amount of drug used during the relapse (Jaffe et al., 1996; O'Malley et al., 1992), duration of relapse (O'Malley et al., 1992; Volpicelli et al., 1992), craving under general conditions (Volpicelli et al., 1992); and subjective high experienced with drug ingestion (Volpicelli, Watson, King, Sherman, & O'Brien, 1995; Volpicelli et al., 1997). Although Volpicelli et al. (1992; 1997) did include a mood scale in their studies, the dependent variables that are lacking in these studies include some of the additional known effects of down-regulating the mesolimbic, mesocortical pathways operating in drug-sensitization: lethargy, amotivation, apathy, and subtle changes in behavior when working for reward. Others have also noted an absence of evaluation of these effects in studies evaluating drugs aimed at decreasing relapse (Wilcox & McMillen, 1998). Yet, depression, anxiety, and irritability are listed as side effects in the Physician's Desk Reference for Trexan (long acting naloxone). It should also be recalled that naloxone is used by neurobiologists to induce conditioned place aversion (Berridge & Robinson, 1998); that it diminishes the reward value of water as well as alcohol (Williams & Wood, 1999); that it can abrogate the positive effects of prior therapeutic desensitization (Arntz, Merckelbach, & deJong, 1993; Merluzzi, Taylor, Boltwood, & Gotestam, 1991); and that it can block the stress reducing effects of endogenous opioids (Bandura, O'Leary, Taylor, Gautheir, & Gossard, 1987; Bruehl et al., 1994; McCubbin et al., 1996). Perhaps in evaluating drugs used to prevent relapse, we should extend our vision to include the total function of the individual.

CONCLUSIONS

Neurobiological research has further refined the view of dopamine structures in the ventral tegmental area which projects to the nucleus accumbens. Whereas these structures had previously been viewed as "pleasure centers," new findings indicate that these structures are not about the experience of pleasure. These structures underpin a wide range of motivated behaviors and many types of wanting. They are active when organisms work for food and water. Recent research suggests that they are active when prairie voles, a monogamous species, form attachments to their mates (Gingrich, Liu, Cascio, Wang, & Insel, 2000). While the dopaminergic structures are linked to motivation and wanting, they are independent from enjoyment. The new discovery for addiction is that these same structures are activated through ingestion of drugs of abuse. Once activated by the drug, drug-seeking behavior and continued activation of dopaminergic structures follow. Thus, the subjective phenomenon of loss of control is mirrored in measurable physiological activity. Strongly motivated, drug-seeking behavior, which cannot be explained in terms of the pleasure resulting from the behavior, now has a physiological explanation.

REFERENCES

American Psychiatric Association: Work Group on Nicotine Dependence. (1996). Practice guidelines for the treatment of patients with nicotine dependence. *American Journal of Psychiatry, 153,* S1-S31.

Arntz, A., Merckelbach, H., & de Jong, P. (1993). Opioid antagonist affects behavioral effects of exposure in vivo. *Journal of Consulting and Clinical Psychology, 61,* 865-870.

Ball, S. A., & Zuckerman, M. (1992). Sensation seeking and selective attention: Focused and divided attention on a dichotic listening task. *Journal of Personality and Social Psychology, 63,* 825-831.

Bandura, A., O'Leary, A., Taylor, C. B., Gautheir, J., & Gossard, D. (1987). Perceived self-efficacy and pain control: Opioid and non-opioid mechanisms. *Journal of Personality and Social Psychology, 53,* 563-571.

Berridge, K. C. (1999). Pleasure, pain, desire, and dread: Hidden core processes of emotion. In D. Kahneman, E. Diener, & N. Schwarz (Eds.) *Well-being: The foundations of hedonic psychology,* (pp. 523-557). New York: Russell Sage Foundation.

Berridge, K. C., & Robinson, T. E. (1998). What is the role of dopamine in reward: Hedonic impart, reward learning, or incentive salience? *Brain Research Review, 28,* 309-369.

Bevins, R. A. & Bardo, M. T. (1998). Morphine-conditioned changes in locomotor activity: Role of the conditioned stimulus. *Experimental and Clinical Psychopharmacology, 6,* 131-138.

Bouton, M. E. (2000). A learning theory perspective on lapse, relapse, and maintenance of behavior change. *Health Psychology, 19,* S57-S63.

Bruehl, S., McCubbin, J. A., Wilson, J. F., Montgomery, T., Ibarra, P., & Carlson, C. R. (1994). Coping styles, opioid blockade, and cardiovascular response to stress. *Journal of Behavioral Medicine, 17,* 25-40.

Childress, A. R., Mozley, P. D., McElgin, W., Fitzgerald, J., Reivich, M., & O'Brien, C. P. (1999). Limbic activation during cue-induced cocaine craving. *American Journal of Psychiatry, 156,* 11-18.

Disney, E. R., Elkins, I. J., McGure, M., & Iacono, W. G. (1999). Effects of ADHD, conduct disorder, and gender on substance use and abuse in adolescence. *American Journal of Psychiatry, 156*, 1515-1521.

Donohew, R. L., Hoyle, R. H., Clayton, R. R., Skinner, W. F., Colon, S. E., & Rice, R. E. (1999). Sensation seeking and drug use by adolescents and their friends: Models for marijuana and alcohol. *Journal of Studies on Alcohol, 60*, 622-631.

Extein, I., & Dackis, C. A. (1987). Brain mechanisms in cocaine dependency. In A. M. Washton & M. S. Gold (Eds.) *Cocaine: A Clinician's Handbook*, (pp. 73-84). New York: Guilford Press.

Finn, P. R., Sharkansky, E. J., Brandt, K. M., & Turcotte, N. (2000). The effects of familial risk, personality, and expectancies on alcohol use and abuse. *Journal of Abnormal Psychology, 109*, 122-133.

Flannery, B. A., Volpicelli, J. R., & Pettinati, H. M. (1999). Psychometric properties of the Penn Alcohol Craving Scale. *Alcoholism: Clinical and Experimental Research, 23*, 1289-1295.

Gingrich, B., Liu, Y., Cascio, C., Wang, Z., & Insel, T. R. (2000). Dopamine D2 receptors in the nucleus accumbens are important for social attachment in female prairie voles. *Behavioral Neuroscience, 114*, 173-183.

Grilly, D. M. (1998). *Drugs and Human Behavior* (3rd ed.). Needham Heights, MA: Allyn & Bacon.

Hill, S. Y., & Yuan, H. (1999). Familial density of alcoholism and onset of adolescent drinking. *Journal of Studies on Alcohol, 60*, 7-17.

Hooks, M. S., Jones, G. H., Neill, D. B., & Justice, Jr., J. B. (1992). Individual differences in amphetamine sensitization: Dose-dependent effects. *Pharmacology, Biochemistry, and Behavior, 41*, 203-210.

Hooks, M. S., Jones, G. H., Smith, A. D., Neill, D. B., & Justice, Jr., J. B. (1991). Individual differences in locomotor activity and sensitization. *Pharmacology, Biochemistry, and Behavior, 38*, 467-470.

Jaffe, A. J., Rounsaville, B., Chang, G., Schottenfeld, R. S., Meyer, R. E., & O'Malley, S. S. (1996). Naltrexone, relapse prevention, and supportive therapy with alcoholics: An analysis of patient treatment matching. *Journal of Consulting and Clinical Psychology, 64*, 1044-1053.

Jorenby, D. E., Smith, S. S., Fiore, M. C., Hurt, R. D., Offord, K. P., Croghan, I. T., Hays, J. T., Lewis, S. F., & Baker, T. B. (1995). Varying nicotine patch dose and type of smoking counseling. *Journal of the American Medical Association, 274*, 1347-1352.

Kilby, M. M., Downey, K., & Breslau, N. (1998). Predicting the emergence and persistence of alcohol dependence in young adults: The role of expectancy and other risk factors. *Experimental and Clinical Psychopharmacology, 6*, 149-156.

Killeen, P. (1975). On the temporal control of behavior. *Psychological Review, 82*, 89-115.

Killeen, P., Hanson, S., & Osborn, S. (1978). Arousal: Its genesis and manifestation as a response rate. *Psychological Review, 85*, 571-581.

Kirk, S. A., & Kutchins, H. (1992). *The selling of the DSM: The Rhetoric of Science in Psychiatry*. New York: Aldine de Gruyter.

Knoblich, G., Curtis, D., Faustman, W. O., Zarcone, V., Stewart, S., Mefford, I., & King, R. (1992). Increased CSF HVA with craving in long-term abstinent cocaine abusers. *Biological Psychiatry, 32*, 96-100.

Kosten, T., Silverman, D. G., Fleming, J., Kosten, T. A., Gawin, F. H., Compton, M., Jatlow, P., & Byck, R. (1992). Intravenous cocaine challenges during naltrexone maintenance: A preliminary study. *Biological Psychiatry, 32*, 543-548.

Lamb, R. J., Preston, K. L., Schindler, C., Meisch, R. A., Davis, F., Katz, J. L., Henningfield, J. E., & Goldberg, S. R. (1991). The reinforcing and subjective effects of morphine in post-addicts: A dose-response study. *Journal of Pharmacology and Experimental Therapeutics, 259*, 1165-1173.

Levin, F. R., Evans, S. M., McDowell, D. M., & Kleber, H. D. (1998). Methylphenidate treatment for cocaine abusers with adult attention-deficit/hyperactivity disorder: A pilot study. *Journal of Clinical Psychiatry, 59*, 300-305.

Li, T. K. (2000). Pharmacogenetics of responses to alcohol and genes that influence alcohol drinking (1998 Mark Keller Honorary Lecture). *Journal of Studies on Alcohol, 61*, 5-12.

Li, T. K., Lumeng, L., McBride, W. J., Murphy, J. M., Froehlich, J. C., & Morzorati, S. (1989). Pharmacology of alcohol preference in rodents. In E. Gordis, B. Tabakoff, & M. Linnoila (Eds.) *Alcohol research form bench to bedside* (pp. 73-86). New York: Hawthorne Press.

Lipkus, I. M., Barefoot, J. C., Williams, R. B., & Siegler, I. C. (1994). Personality measures as predictors of smoking initiation and cessation in the UNC Alumni Heart Study. *Health Psychology, 13*, 149-155.

Littrell, J. (1991a). *Understanding and treating alcoholism: An empirically based clinician's handbook for the treatment of alcoholism.* Hillsdale, NJ: Lawrence Erlbaum & Associates.

Littrell, J. (1991b). *Understanding and treating alcoholism: Biological, psychological, and social aspects of alcohol consumption and abuse.* Hillsdale, NJ: Lawrence Erlbaum & Associates.

McCubbin, J. A., Wilson, J. F., Bruehl, S. Ibarra, P., Carlson, C. R., Norton, J. A., & Colclough, G. W. (1996). Relaxation and blood pressure response to stress. *Journal of Consulting and Clinical Psychology, 64*, 593-601.

Merluzzi, T. V., Taylor, C. B., Boltwood, T. B., & Gotestam, K. G. (1991). Aerobic fitness and opioidergic inhibition of cardiovascular stress reactivity. *Psychophysiology, 29*, 687-697.

O'Malley, S. S., Croop, R. S., Wroblewski, J. M., Labriola, D. F., & Volpicelli, J. R. (1995). Naltrexone in the treatment of alcohol dependence: A combined analysis of two trials. *Psychiatric Annals, 25*, 681-688.

O'Malley, S. S., Jaffe, A. J., Chang, G., Schottenfeld, R. S., Meyer, R. E., & Rounsaville, B. (1992). Naltrexone and coping skills therapy for alcohol dependence: A controlled study. *Archives of General Psychiatry, 49*, 881-887.

Osborn, E., Grey, C., & Reznikoff, M. (1986). Psychosocial adjustment, modality choice, and outcome in naltrexone versus methadone treatment. *American Journal of Drug and Alcohol Abuse, 12*, 383-388.

Piasecki, T. M., Niaura, R., Shadel, W. G., Abrams, D., Goldstein, M., Fiore, M. C., & Baker, T. B. (2000). Smoking withdrawal dynamics in unaided quitters. *Journal of Abnormal Psychology, 109*, 74-86.

Post, R. M., & Weiss, S. R. B. (1988). Sensitization and kindling: Implications for the evolution of psychiatric symptomatology. In P.W. Kalivas & C. D. Barnes (Eds.), *Sensitization in the Nervous System*, pp. 257-291. Caldwell, NJ: Telford Press.

Rada, P. V., Mark, G. P., & Hoebel, B. G. (1998). Dopamine release in the nucleus accumbens by hypothalamic stimulation-escape behavior. *Brain Research, 782,* 228-234.

Robbins, S. J., & Ehrman, R. N. (1998). Cocaine use is associated with increased craving in outpatient cocaine abusers. *Experimental and Clinical Psychopharmacology, 6,* 217-224.

Robbins, T. W., & Everitt, B. J. (1996). Neurobehavioral mechanisms of reward and motivation. *Current Opinion in Neurobiology, 6,* 228-236.

Robinson, T. E. (1988). Stimulant drugs and stress: Factors influencing individual differences in the susceptibility to sensitization. In P.W. Kalivas & C. D. Barnes (Eds.), *Sensitization in the Nervous System,* (pp. 145-173). Caldwell, NJ: Telford Press.

Robinson, T. E., & Berridge, K. C. (1993). The neural basis of drug craving: An incentive-sensitization theory of addiction. *Brain Research Reviews, 18,* 247-291.

Sabol, S. Z., Nelson, M. L., Fisher, C., Gunzerath, L., Brody, C. L., Hu, S., Sirota, L. A., Marcus, S. E., Greenberg, B. D., Lucas, F. R., Benjamin, J., Murphy, D. L., & Hamer, D. H. (1999). A genetic association for cigarette smoking behavior. *Health Psychology, 18,* 7-13.

Salamone, J. D. (1992). Complex motor and sensorimotor functions of the striatal and accumbens dopamine: Involvement in instrumental behavior processes. *Psychopharmacology, 107,* 160-174.

Salamone, J. D., Aberman, J. E., Sokolowski, J. D., & Cousins, M. S. (1999). Nucleus accumbens dopamine and rate of responding: Neurochemical and behavioral studies. *Psychobiology, 27,* 236-247.

Salamone, J. D., Cousins, M. S., & Snyder, B. J. (1997). Behavioral functions of the Nucleus Accumbens dopamine: Empirical and conceptual problems with the anhedonia hypothesis. *Neuroscience and Biobehavioral Reviews, 21,* 341-359.

Salamone, J. D., Zigmond, M. J., & Stricker, E. M. (1990). Characterization of impaired feeding behavior in rats given haldoperiodol or dopamine-depleting brain lesions. *Neuroscience, 39,* 17-24.

Sandbak, T., Murison, R., Sarviharju, M., & Hyytia, P. (1998). Defensive burying and stress gastric erosions in alcohol-preferring AA and alcohol-avoiding ANA rats. *Alcoholism: Clinical and Experimental Research, 22,* 2050-2054.

Schulteis, G., & Koob, G. F. (1996). Reinforcement processes in opiate addiction: A homeostatic model. *Neurochemical Research, 21,* 1437-1454.

Shaham, Y., Rajabi, H., & Stewart, J. (1996). Relapse to heroin-seeking in rats under opioid maintenance: The effects of stress, heroin priming, and withdrawal. *Journal of Neuroscience, 16,* 1957-1963.

Smith, R. E., Ptacek, J. T., & Smoll, F. L. (1992). Sensation seeking, stress, and adolescent injuries: A test-of stress buffering, risk-taking, and coping skills hypotheses. *Journal of Personality and Social Psychology, 62,* 1016-1024.

Stewart, J., & Vezina, P. (1988). Conditioning and behavioral sensitization. In P.W. Kalivas & C. D. Barnes (Eds), *Sensitization in the Nervous System*, (pp. 207-224). Caldwell, NJ: Telford Press.

Tamerin, J. S., Weiner, S., & Mendelson, J. H. (1970). Alcoholics' expectancies during intoxication. *American Journal of Psychiatry*, *126*, 1679-1704.

Volpicelli, R., Alterman, A. I., Hayashida, M., & O'Brien, C. P. (1992). Naltrexone in the treatment of alcohol dependence. *Archives of General Psychiatry*, *49*, 876-880.

Volpicelli, J. R., Clay, K. L., Rhines, J. S., Volpicelli, L. A., Alterman, A. I., & O'Brien, C. P. (1997). Naltrexone and alcohol dependence: Role of subject compliance. *Archives of General Psychiatry*, *54*, 737-742.

Volpicelli, J. R., Watson, N. T., King, A. C., Sherman, C. E., & O'Brien, C. P. (1995). Effect of naltrexone on alcohol "high" in humans. *American Journal of Psychiatry*, *152*, 613-615.

Walsh, S. L., Sullivan, J. T., Preston, K. L., Garner, J. E., & Bieglow, G. E. (1996). Effects of naltrexone on response to intravenous cocaine, hydromorphone, and their combination in humans. *Journal of Pharmacology and Experimental Therapeutics*, *279*, 524-538.

Watson, D., Clark, L. A., McIntyre, C. W., & Hamaker, S. (1992). Affect, personality, and social activity. *Journal of Personality and Social Psychology*, *63*, 1011-1025.

Wikler, A. (1973). Dynamics of drug dependence: Implications of a conditioning theory for research and treatment. *Archives of General Psychiatry*, *28*, 611-616.

Wilcox, R. E., & McMillen, B. A. (1998). The rationale use of drugs as therapeutic agents for the treatment of the alcoholisms. *Alcohol*, *15*, 161-177.

Williams, K. L., & Woods, J. H. (1999). Naltrexone reduces ethanol-and/or water-reinforced responding in rhesus monkeys: Effect depends upon ethanol concentration. *Alcoholism: Clinical and Experimental Research*, *23*, 1462-1467.

Wise, R. A. (1999). Cognitive factors in addiction and nucleus accumbens function: Some hints from rodent models. *Psychobiology*, *27*, 300-310.

Wise, R. A., & Bozarth, M. A. (1987). A psychomotor stimulant theory of addiction. *Psychological Review*, *94*, 469-492.

Wise, R. A., & Rompre, P. P. (1989). Brain dopamine and reward. *Annual Review of Psychology*, *40*, 191-225.

Impact of Drugs and Alcohol on the Brain Through the Life Cycle: Knowledge for Social Workers

Efrain C. Azmitia

SUMMARY. This article discusses the impact of alcohol and other drugs on the brain during five stages of the life cycle: perinatal (pregnancy-2 years), childhood (2-12 years), adolescence (13-21), adulthood (22-50), and senior (50+). Alcohol and psychotropic drugs act through specific chemicals in the brain called neurotransmitters. Neurotransmitters have two main functions in the brain: mediate electrical transmission (synaptic activity) and promote growth (trophic activity). The trophic activity results in a neuron increasing its size and the complexity of its branches (dendrites). The ability of drugs and alcohol to influence neuronal growth (neuroplasticity) has unique consequences in children, adults, and seniors. Knowledge of such biological principles as developmental critical period, age-related cortical shrinkage and steroid-induced neuronal growth is presented in the context of alcohol and other drug abuse. A few suggestions are made for developing

Efrain C. Azmitia, PhD, is Professor of Biology and Psychiatry, Center for Neural Science, New York University, 10-09 Main Building, 100 Washington Square East, New York, NY 10003 (E-mail: efrain.azmitia@nyu.edu).

This article is based on a presentation for the National Association of Social Workers Alcohol and Other Drug Section and the New York City Chapter of NASW Addiction Institute, May 7, 1999, New York City.

[Haworth co-indexing entry note]: "Impact of Drugs and Alcohol on the Brain Through the Life Cycle: Knowledge for Social Workers." Azmitia, Efrain C. Co-published simultaneously in *Journal of Social Work Practice in the Addictions* (The Haworth Social Work Practice Press, an imprint of The Haworth Press, Inc.) Vol. 1, No. 3, 2001, pp. 41-63; and: *Neurobiology of Addictions: Implications for Clinical Practice* (ed: Richard T. Spence, Diane M. DiNitto, and Shulamith Lala Ashenberg Straussner) The Haworth Social Work Practice Press, an imprint of The Haworth Press, Inc., 2001, pp. 41-63. Single or multiple copies of this article are available for a fee from The Haworth Document Delivery Service [1-800-342-9678, 9:00 a.m. - 5:00 p.m. (EST). E-mail address: getinfo@haworthpressinc.com].

41

new treatment strategies based on the inherent dynamics of the brain during the life cycle. *[Article copies available for a fee from The Haworth Document Delivery Service: 1-800-342-9678. E-mail address: <getinfo@haworthpressinc.com> Website: <http://www.HaworthPress.com> © 2001 by The Haworth Press, Inc. All rights reserved.]*

KEYWORDS. Neuroplasticity, fetus, children, adolescence, cocaine, alcohol, risk, self-medication

INTRODUCTION

The typical concepts that most people have of the brain are wrong. They falsely believe that the brain is like a computer composed of hard-wired permanent connections. Instead, the structure of the brain is *plastic*, meaning that it can change. Another common belief is that we use only 10% of our brain. In fact, we use 100% since brain cells must be constantly active to sustain life. Yet another misunderstanding is that brain cells die in alarming numbers as we age, especially when we consume alcohol or drugs. A more accurate view is that the brain contains a large, relatively fixed number of neurons, which are constantly changing, either growing or retracting in size and complexity. Careful morphometric studies show no loss of neurons in the cortex of alcoholics (Harding, Wong, Svoboda, Kril, & Halliday, 1997) and of seniors (Long, Mouton, Jucker, & Ingram, 1999). Likewise, drugs of abuse have little effect on the death of neurons, but a significant effect on the number of connections between dendrites and axons (*synapses*) and subsequently, on the size of the brain. This process, whereby neuronal size and shape are dynamic in the mature brain, is termed *neuroplasticity*. As a consequence, connections between neurons are in constant flux and stored memories are fluid and changeable, not fixed and exact.

This biological view of the brain has important conceptual and clinical consequences because it makes us aware that our environment and experience are constantly modifying our neurons. Alcohol and other drugs (AOD) interact mainly through the chemical systems of the brain (*neurotransmitters*), and influence their activity. AOD may change the levels of the neurotransmitters released by the neuron (see Figure 1). Conversely many drugs act, not by modifying the levels of the chemicals, but on the cellular targets of the neurotransmitters (*receptors*). These processes in neurotransmitter action are interrelated and are precisely controlled by feedback mechanisms. Thus, if a drug stimulates a receptor, the reaction is to reduce the number or sensitivity of the receptors in order to compensate for the increase in activity and establish the prior level of functioning. This drive to maintain equilibrium is termed *ho-*

FIGURE 1. Neuronal Functions and Sites of Drug Action

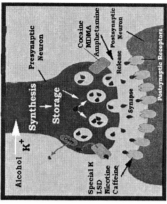

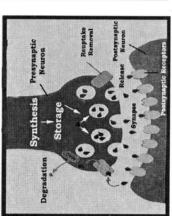

A. A neuron performs many specialized functions. A synapse is a specialized contact between two neurons. The presynaptic neuron synthesizes a neurotransmitter and stores it in vesicles. The vesicles release the neurotransmitter which acts on postsynaptic receptors. The neurotransmitter is removed from the synapse by reuptake protein. If the levels of neurotransmitters increase inside the presynaptic neuron, this chemical can be degraded and removed. Receptors are proteins located on the membrane of the cells which detect the presence of the chemical outside of the cells, in the extracellular space known as the neurophil.

B. Ecstasy (MDMA), cocaine, and methamphetamine block the reuptake and stimulate release of monoaminergic neurons (serotonin, dopamine, and norepinephrine). Nicotine and LSD stimulate (agonist) specific receptors on the postsynaptic neurons. Caffeine and ketamine (known as Special-K) block (act as antagonist) specific receptors. Alcohol modifies ion movement through specific channels and indirectly influences neurotransmitter release.

meostasis. Understanding this homeostatic principle is crucial to an appreciation of the consequence of AOD abuse on long-term brain health.

This article reviews the actions and consequences of drug and alcohol abuse on neuroplasticity during five stages of the life cycle: perinatal development, childhood, adolescence, adulthood, and old age. Table 1 provides a summary of the major changes in brain growth and maturation occurring during each of these periods. This view, based on neuroplasticity, provides a dynamic, biological view of the long-term consequence of drug and alcohol abuse on brain development and functioning. It may shed new light on the mechanism of addiction and how it might be treated.

BASIC PRINCIPLES OF NEUROSCIENCE AND BRAIN PLASTICITY

The numerous neurons in the brain (approximately 10^{12} cells) are separate units of life capable of living in isolation. In the brain, these individual neurons influence each other by releasing concentrated packages of neurotransmitters. Brain neurotransmitters are common chemicals such as glycine, glutamate, GABA, serotonin and dopamine, which are found throughout the body, in all animals and plants. In the brain, these same chemicals are made and stored in large quantities by specialized neurons and can be released in *vesicles* (membrane packages) to influence a neighboring neuron and glial cell. The *glial cells* supply the neurons with glucose (for energy) and also secrete proteins, which can influence the growth of neurons. These non-neuronal cells can be altered by AOD and in human alcoholics show dramatic changes (Korbo, 1999). The specialized space between two adjoining neurons is termed the synapse. Neurotransmitters are released from the pre-synaptic neuron and quickly diffuse across the narrow synaptic gap to interact with receptors situated on the post-synaptic neurons, or cells. Presynaptic neurons have specific proteins on their surface, which can *reuptake* (reabsorb) the chemicals from the synapse. Most abused drugs affect brain activity by interfering with these basic mechanisms of neurotransmitter function impacting the number and sensitivity of receptors, or on the release and reuptake of neurotransmitters, with important consequence to the biology of the brain.

If the effects of drugs were immediate and transient, like electrical flow through a circuit in a computer, no long-term consequences of drug use might be expected. However, the brain is a closed biological system of living cells. The relatively stable interactions between neurons are established during the life of a person, and the basic organization relies on an evolutionary blueprint that has taken over a billion years to achieve. Whenever one chemical system is activated, it has an immediate effect on millions of other cells. Afterwards,

TABLE 1. Impact of Alcohol and Other Drugs During the Life Cycle

Life-Cycle Period	Brain Anatomy[1]	Brain Chemical[2]	Exogenous Substances[3]	Neuroplasticity[4]	Physiological & Psychological Effects[5]	Biological & Medical Actions[6]
Perinatal Fetus-2 Years	Primitive, Immature Cortex	Very High Levels and Very High Receptors	Alcohol, Cocaine, Nicotine	Very Rapid, Development of Major Structures and Connections	Withdrawn, Agitated, Crying, Retardation	Spontaneous Abortion, Premature Birth, Immature Cortex
Children 2-12 Years	Limbic Dominant	High Levels and High Receptors	Alcohol, Inhalants, Caffeine	Rapid, Stress Hormone Responsive	Hyperactive, Aggressive, Impulsive, ADD	Decreased Limbic Cortex
Adolescents 13-21 Years	Limbic/Frontal Balance	High Levels and Moderate Receptors	Alcohol, Nicotine, Marijuana, Hallucinogens, Ecstasy	Rapid, Sex Hormone Responsive	Risk-Behavior, Sex Differences	Increased Limbic and Reduced Frontal Cortex
Adults 22-50 Years	Frontal Dominant	Moderate Levels and Variable Receptors	Alcohol, Marijuana, Cocaine, Barbiturates, Tranquilizers	Intermediate, Cortical Regression, Stress Hormone Responsive	Self-Medication, Anxiety	Reduced Limbic and Increased Frontal Cortex
Seniors 51 + Years	Limbic and Frontal Reduction	Low Levels and Low Receptors	Alcohol, Depressants, Narcotics	Slow, Retraction, Degeneration, Reduced Sex Hormones	Withdrawn, Agitated, Dementia, Emotional	Reduced Cortex

The life cycle is divided into five periods, with flexible age limits.
1. Brain anatomy considers mainly the changes in cortex, of which the Limbic System (hippocampus, amygdala, and temporal) is the emotional center and the Frontal Cortex (actually the prefrontal area anterior to the primary motor area) is the executive center.
2. Brain chemicals are principally the monoamines (serotonin, dopamine, and norepinephrine) and acetylcholine. The value (high to low) is an indication of their fiber density, chemical level, or receptor amounts per unit weight.
3. Exogenous substances are alcohol and other drug (AOD) of choice obtained from national survey data. In perinatal stage, it refers to exposure through ingestion by the pregnant mother. Note: Alcohol is a choice for all periods.
4. Neuroplasticity considers the viability of growth factors and the ability of neurons to change their morphology and connections.
5. Physiological and psychological effects include physiological and behavioral responses, outcomes or motivations.
6. Biological and medical effects are limited to actions in the cortex, except in perinatal period.

there is a reactive period when these systems adjust their chemical levels and receptor function to accommodate the changes in activity; the more pronounced the change, the more dramatic the response. These biochemical changes can last for days, and are primarily responsible for the changes in mood seen several days after drug exposure. These dynamic shifts are accompanied by changes in the growth of the individual cells, a process of neuroplasticity, that leads to modifications in the brain's size, shape and function (see Figure 2). These structural changes can last for weeks and months, or become permanent alterations.

IMPACT OF AOD ON THE PERINATAL STAGE OF DEVELOPMENT

The effects of alcohol and cocaine on fetal development are described below. However, most of the effects of drugs and alcohol on the fetus are not apparent by conventional tests. Subtle changes in brain organization or neurotransmitter levels can result in long-lasting consequences for the child, possibly lasting his/her lifetime. The number of preschool children in the U.S. at biological risk and social disadvantage produced by exposure to drugs is believed to be large. In a study of 309 women at an inner city family planning center in Philadelphia, over 15% of the women had alcohol or another drug in their urine (Harwell, Spence, Sands, & Iguchi, 1996). In a more recent review, Msall, Bier, LaGasse, Tremont, and Lester (1998) reported that 20% of newborns were exposed to alcohol and 10% were exposed to other drugs.

The development of the brain depends on the proper neurons being in the correct place at the appropriate time. Thus, exposing a fetal brain to drugs can disrupt the chemical balance (*homeostasis*) between neurons at a critical time and produce changes in subsequent growth of brain connections lasting the entire life of the child. The fundamental organization of the brain occurs rapidly. Within the four weeks from fertilization, the human fetus has formed its major brain regions: spinal cord, brainstem and forebrain. Within eight weeks, some neurons are already producing neurotransmitters like serotonin and dopamine, chemicals that promote brain growth and maturation. The early appearance of these chemicals, and their receptors, helps establish the framework for future maturation of the brain and of the spinal cord (the central nervous system, CNS). These biological events occur before synaptic contacts are fully established and proceed for an additional 30 weeks (seven months) in an environment protected by the safety of the womb.

Can the placenta protect the growing fetus from foreign chemicals? The fetal CNS has few of the protections afforded the adult CNS. The *blood-brain barrier*, which prevents large molecules and charged chemicals from reaching

FIGURE 2. Impact of Prenatal Exposure to Cocaine

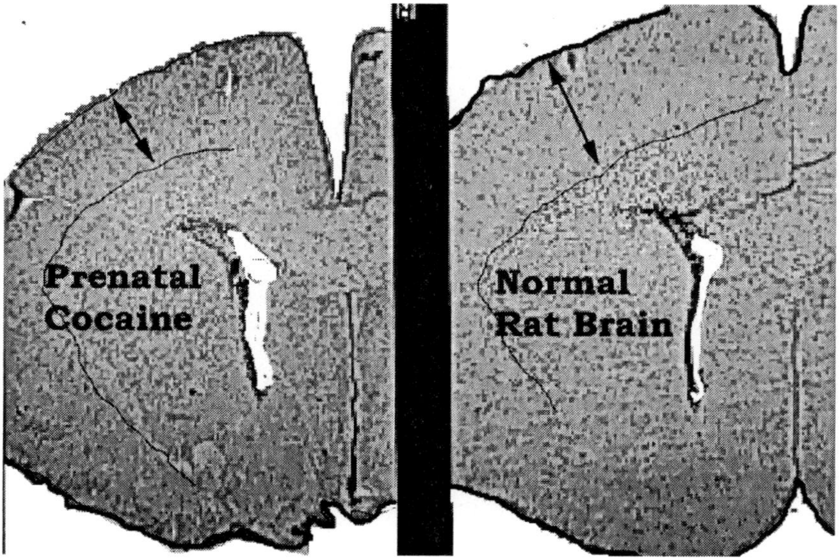

These pictures are from a study in which a group of pregnant rats were administered cocaine for two weeks prior to giving birth. The pups at one week of age were perfused and brain slices were made through the brain. Note the dramatic reduction in cortical thickness in the rat pups treated prenatally with cocaine (left) compared to age-matched pups (right). Source: Akbari et al., 1994.

CNS neurons, does not form until several months after birth. The axons of neurons are naked and not yet surrounded by myelin from specialized glial cells (termed oligodendroglial cells). The fetal liver and kidney are immature and ineffective at detoxifying poisons, so that drugs remain in the body of the fetus and newborn for longer periods of time. Studies show that cocaine has a half-life of 16 hours in a newborn baby; this value decreases to 11.2 hours during the first week of life (Dempsey et al., 1999), compared to 2.5 hours in adults (Taylor, Estevez, Englert, & Ho, 1976). In addition, the fetal brain is more sensitive to drugs. There are more receptors for key chemicals involved in drugs of abuse (e.g., serotonin and dopamine) at birth, than later in life. In fact, receptors for dopamine (D1) in the forebrain are 7-15 times greater around birth (perinatal) than in adult brain regions (Boyson & Adams, 1997).

AOD abuse is associated with a premature termination of pregnancy (spontaneous abortions). A study of a large number of adolescents and adult women (14-40 years of age) in an inner city hospital emergency unit found that drugs ingested by the mother may increase the risk of spontaneous abortions and structural abnormalities in newborn babies (Ness, 1999). The study followed 400 women who had spontaneous abortions either at study entry or during follow-up, which lasted until 22 weeks of gestation. Among those who had spontaneous abortions, 28.9% used cocaine and 34.6% smoked cigarettes, as compared with 20.5% and 21.8%, respectively, of the females who did not have a spontaneous abortion. Therefore, there is an overall, significant increase of 24% in the risk of spontaneous abortion related to cocaine or tobacco use.

Studies of both animals and humans show the destructive impact of maternal cocaine abuse on newborns. The early warnings of the dangers of prenatal cocaine exposure effects on fetal growth came from scientists working with pregnant rats in the controlled environment of the laboratory. Researchers found that pups born after cocaine exposure had a low birth weight and smaller brains (microencephally). In these animals, the neurons, which make serotonin, had shorter projections. Glial cells, which support the growth of neurons, produced less of a trophic factor, called S100ß (Akbari, Whitaker-Azmitia, & Azmitia, 1994). Moreover, the thickness of the cerebral cortex was significantly reduced. As a consequence, these animals had delayed developmental milestones, such as teeth eruption and eye opening. These results paralleled the clinical findings on human babies.

Babies exposed to cocaine prenatally, unpleasantly called "crack babies," are at risk for premature birth, low birth weight and smaller head circumference, and to be socially withdrawn from their parents and others (Zuckerman et al., 1989). In another study, 240 infants (104 control and 136 cocaine exposed as determined by radioimmunoassay of maternal hair) were examined shortly after birth (Chiriboga, Brust, Bateman, & Hauser, 1999). Cocaine exposure during the last trimester was compared with unexposed controls. Cocaine-exposed infants exhibited higher rates of intrauterine growth retardation (24% vs. 8%), small head circumference (20% vs. 5%) and neurological abnormalities such as global hypertonia (32% vs. 11%), coarse tremor (40% vs. 15%), and extensor leg posture (20% vs. 4%). Overall, children with prenatal cocaine exposure show higher rates of impairments in fetal head growth and abnormalities of muscle tone, movements, and posture. These babies are not only born less mature, but they may also be at increased risk for illness. Studies have shown that children exposed to cocaine prenatally also have a suppressed immune system (Karlix et al., 1998). In addition, newborns whose mothers who had positive urine assays for marijuana had a 79-g lower birth weight (p = 0.04) and a 0.5-cm decrement in length (p = 0.02) when compared to infants of women who did not test positive for marijuana (Zuckerman et al., 1989).

Alcohol is the most abused substance in the U.S. today. Unfortunately for fetuses and babies, the liver enzyme, which metabolizes alcohol, is fairly immature until after birth. A pregnant woman who drinks exposes a fetus to a toxic substance that its young body cannot metabolize. One of the consequences of maternal alcohol use is an increased risk that the fetus is spontaneously aborted. Those fetuses which survive prenatal alcohol exposure may have Fetal Alcohol Syndrome (FAS), the number one cause of mental retardation in children. FAS babies show heightened agitation and crying. The babies are developmentally delayed in motor, cognitive, and social skills. The actions of alcohol are complex, and include strong interactions with the K+ (potassium ion) channels in neurons and glial cells. In animal studies, there is decreased serotonin in rats prenatally exposed to alcohol (Tajuddin & Druse, 1999), and this in turn results in a loss of a trophic factor, S100ß, produced by glial cells. This factor was also reduced after prenatal cocaine exposure, and its reduction during brain development might help explain the delay in neuronal maturation occurring after AOD exposure.

IMPACT OF AOD DURING CHILDHOOD

Children exposed to drugs prenatally are at greater risk of problems during their childhood. The child can be hyperactive and aggressive, or she/he can be quiet and withdrawn. The unusual behaviors may reflect an altered brain chemistry and anatomy. At three years of age, prenatal cocaine use by a mother was a significant predictor of smaller head circumference and of a lower composite score on the Stanford-Binet Intelligence Scale (Richardson, 1998). Prenatal cocaine use was also associated with temperamental differences at one and three years of age, and with behavior problems at three years. In one study, 199 subjects (98 cocaine-exposed and 101 unexposed) returned to the hospital at age two for assessment of motor development. Compared with control subjects, the cocaine-exposed group performed significantly less well on both the fine and the gross motor development indices (Arendt, Angelopoulos, Salvator, & Singer, 1999).

The key to understanding these long-term consequences of prenatal AOD exposure on children is that the disruption occurs at critical periods during early development. A critical period is a time of development when several systems interact causing changes in their maturation or growth patterns. These interacting systems, in turn, will affect other systems. In particular, cocaine, cigarette smoking, or alcohol exposure arrests the maturation of a select group of neuronal systems (e.g., monoaminergic and cholinergic). The problem becomes compounded since these neurons have direct trophic effects on their target cells which are likewise either arrested or stimulated, and so on down the line. Cocaine, given prenatally but not postnatally in rats, arrests the growth of monoaminergic fibers, especially serotonin (Akbari & Azmitia, 1992). The number of serotonergic fibers in the cortex of cocaine-exposed fetuses is significantly reduced at birth. The reduced growth of serotonergic fibers can, in turn, slow down the maturation of the neurons and glial cells in the developing cortex at critical periods. Nicotine, the active drug in cigarettes, reduces cholinergic development in rats exposed prenatally (Zahalka et al., 1992) and leads to a reduction in the thickness of the cortex (Roy & Sabherwal, 1994). The effects of nicotine in animals are strongly dependent on when the drug is administered (Aramakis, Hsieh, Leslie, & Metherate, 2000).

It might be expected that the slowing of brain maturation would be rectified (reversed) as the child grows and his brain is allowed to mature in the absence of the drugs. To some degree, this does happen. The stunted neurons not only recover their normal growth rate, but also appear to grow faster than normal once cocaine is removed. In animals, after several months of life, the serotonergic innervation of the cortex appears to normalize. But the interactions between neuronal systems may be permanently altered because some of the neurons were not ready earlier when another group of neurons reached out to establish a connection.[1] Likewise, children exposed to drugs prenatally are vulnerable to missing key developmental milestones during their early years. For such children, the connections between appropriate brain regions may not be as well established as in other children. These children could be more easily distracted, and be more socially unstable (either by being disruptive or withdrawn). In a study of the long-term consequences of fetal exposure to nicotine, the offspring of mothers who smoked at least ten cigarettes a day during pregnancy were followed for ten years. Boys showed a four-fold increase (400%) in prepubertal conduct disorders (Weissman, Warner, Wickramaratne, & Kandel, 1999). Therefore, children exposed to prenatal AOD may need special postnatal care. A slowing of the demands of schooling and a reduction in stress could allow the brain of these children to slowly re-establish the appropriate connections to meet social demands.

Stress can have an adverse affect on neuronal development. Although drug exposed babies may benefit from a tranquil environment, this is often not the case. Parents who abuse AOD due to stress are also more likely to harm their children after birth (Stranger et al., 1999). Head injury, due to parental neglect or violence, is not uncommon among these children. Moreover, stress to a pregnant woman or during childbirth is suspected of producing lasting changes in the child's behavior. Animal studies have clearly established permanent changes in brain anatomy and chemistry resulting from exposing pregnant rats to stressors. In neonate rats, even a brief separation from the mother is sufficient to alter the number of serotonin receptors, the normal learning curve, and may even shorten the animal's life (Smythe, Rowe, & Meaney, 1994). The power of these early stressors is believed to be principally due to changes in stress hormones or steroid (glucocorticoids) levels during early neuronal growth spurts.

Unlike sex hormones, which increase dramatically at puberty, children from a very early age secrete stress hormones. The stress of maternal separation on the social development of children is well known. However, children whose parents abuse AOD are exposed to many stressors throughout their early years. There is a strong correlation between aggression and addictive behaviors in these children as they age. Studies of cocaine- and opiate-dependent parents in treatment indicate that their children have been abused and exposed to violence in the home (Stanger et al., 1999). This stressful environment on growing children needs to be considered when trying to understand the biological factors that may later influence alcohol and other drug abuse.

Why should stress have an impact on the brain? Research has clearly established that stress hormones, such as glucocorticoids, contribute to the maturation of selective neurons of the emotional centers in the brain, known as the Limbic System. The Limbic System is that part of the brain involved in emotional expression (e.g., mood, aggression, anger). Rats exposed prenatally to glucocorticoids have 80% larger serotonin cell bodies for producing serotonin, which form more elaborate dendritic branches (Azmitia, Liao, & Chen, 1993). The more branches a neuron has, the more connections it seeks to make. Thus, exposure to stress steroids, especially in children, can alter the balance of brain connections by producing an increased demand for new connections within the limbic system. This can influence the activity of these brain centers, by either increasing the number of inhibitory or excitatory connections. Thus, a child exposed to stress may be unusually quiet and withdrawn, or hyperactive and aggressive.

The rapidly growing brain of children exposed to stress steroids can become overly primed to receive sensory stimulation because of altered growth of neuronal branches which seek connections. The most widely abused drug by children (in fact, by all people) is caffeine. Caffeine inhibits neurons which make adenosine, a brain relaxant. Caffeine, therefore, is a very powerful stimulating drug, and children exposed to AOD and/or stress may be particularly vulnerable to the actions of this drug found in high levels in most soda drinks, tea, coffee, chocolate, and energy bars. After caffeine, the drugs most abused by children are alcohol and inhalants, both of which are CNS depressants. It might be argued these drugs are more accessible to children, but it is also consistent with a desire to reduce sensory inputs at a time when sensory overload might be a problem. Furthermore, children suffering from Attention Deficit

Disorder (ADD) tend to abuse cocaine as adults (Kafka & Prentky, 1998). The cause of ADD appears to be caused by developmental problems with the monoamine systems, the very systems that are targeted by cocaine. Interestingly, the most commonly prescribed drug for ADD is Ritalin, a derivative of amphetamine. It provides a good temporary fix, but may not be the best choice for long-term brain repair because it masks the underlying problem.

IMPACT OF AOD ABUSE ON ADOLESCENTS

Children undergo profound physiological changes during puberty (a period also termed adolescence). Boys develop muscles, facial hair, and a deeper voice. Girls develop breasts and begin their menstrual cycle. Both genders experience new sexual urges. The brain, of course, is instrumental at directing these hormonal and behavioral changes by regulating the secretion of key hormones from the hypothalamus and pituitary gland. Inside the brain, select groups of neurons express steroid receptors, which allow them to respond to circulating hormones. Activation of these hormonal receptors has dramatic effects on the growth and maturation of those selected neural systems (Garcia-Segura, Chowen, Parducz, & Naftolin, 1994). During this stage of life, adolescents experiment with new sensations and increase risk-taking behavior.

In general, adolescence is associated with a dramatic increase in drug experimentation. Children at this age desire to try drugs and alcohol, in much the same way they want to listen to new music, wear unique clothes, and explore personal relationships. Current estimates are that over 80% of teenagers have tried alcohol and 50% have tried marijuana while in high school (CASA Survey, 1999). Experimentation with cocaine, ecstasy, hallucinogens, heroin and other drugs is significantly increased during the adolescent period. The most serious problem with infrequent and naive use of AOD is not addiction, but death resulting from an overdose producing respiratory failure, heart attack, hyperthermia, or panic attacks.

Biological predisposition not only makes it more likely a child will try a drug, but also makes the physical dependency on that drug more likely. Some people can regularly use a drug and not develop an abuse pattern. Others develop severe problems with physical dependency within a relatively short period of time. Alcohol is the prime example, but amphetamines and barbiturates show evidence of physical dependency. Even cocaine, which has a very high addiction liability, poses a greater risk in adolescents with ADD than in others. Thus, abuse is a function of both the drug and the biological substrate in the brain. The most vulnerable adolescents are those having prior prenatal exposure to alcohol and other drugs or prior exposure to stressful environments. The problems from early exposure are now combined with the new biological demands imposed on adolescents by hormonal surges. The adolescent daughters of mothers who smoked heavily during pregnancy were 500 times more likely to become drug dependent than controls (Weissman et al., 1999). The influx of potent sex steroids into the brain might exacerbate inappropriate or unbalanced connections established during childhood.

AOD experimentation may be related to risk taking behavior. The drive for heightened sensory stimulation is an aspect of thrill-seeking or risk-taking behavior. These impulsive actions, if overly expressed, are disruptive and may be a warning sign for subsequent AOD usage in children and adolescents. Animal studies have long shown that low brain levels of serotonin produce a marked increase in impulsivity. Rats given drugs to lower serotonin explore their environment more, are easier to startle, and respond more vigorously to painful stimuli (Azmitia, 1978). The opposite findings are true when serotonin is increased with drugs that block reuptake (e.g., Prozac, Zoloft). Human studies demonstrate a correlation between impulsivity and risk taking behavior and drug and alcohol abuse (DuRant et al., 1999). For example, gambling is a high-risk behavior. A study of a large number of adolescents (n = 21,297) from grades 8-12, found 53% reported gambling in the past 12 months, and 7% reported problems attributable to gambling (Proimos, DuRant, Pierce, & Goodman, 1998). Gambling frequency was seen mainly in male teenagers who also use alcohol, marijuana, inhalant, steroids, or other illicit drugs. In addition, teenage gambling was significantly associated with a variety of risk behaviors (such as seatbelt nonuse, threatening others, carrying a weapon, being involved in a fight, and early sexual activity), which included drinking and driving. Boys, in general, show more risk-taking behavior than girls (Schootman, Fuortes, Zwerling, Albanese, & Watson, 1999). AOD abuse is not an isolated behavior in teenagers; many warning signs are more readily apparent.

There are marked sex differences during the adolescent period of experimentation because the brains of boys and girls are continually exposed to different hormones. Estrogen, which greatly increases in young girls, has been shown to stimulate the maturation and connections of neurons in Limbic System centers. Testosterone, produced in greater amounts in boys, is not as beneficial as estrogen to neuronal growth. Thus, puberty is a time of selective brain growth for both sexes and a rearrangement of many brain connections, especially those found within the emotional limbic centers of the brain. Adolescent boys, driven by testosterone, can become more assertive, outgoing and even aggressive (Sanchez-Martin et al., 2000). In animal studies, testosterone administered to male rats results in increased movement and a dramatic rise in aggressiveness. Women also have testosterone in their bodies, and it has been correlated with assertiveness and increased ideation about sex.

These *sex-linked* changes in emotions and thinking are expressions of changes in the size and maturation of key neurons in the brain following steroid exposure and may help explain the gender differences in drug and alcohol abuse. Although approximately the same number of boys and girls smoke cigarettes and drink alcohol, girls are less susceptible than boys to excessive behaviors associated with use (Soyibo & Lee, 1999). In addition, boys are more likely to abuse illicit drugs. A study of 6,711 children ages 11-18 in Spain found that significantly more males than females tried cannabis, cocaine, or heroin (Vega, Alderete, Kolody, & Aguilar-Gaxiola, 1998). Likewise, in a study of Native Americans (Indians), there was no gender difference in those trying marijuana, but males were more likely to use it at a higher rate (Novins & Mitchell, 1998). Girls are also at risk. Girls were 500% more likely to abuse AOD when exposed to mother's cigarette smoking before birth (Weissman et al., 1999). Interestingly, a survey done in England (Henderson, 1993) provides evidence that girls may be more likely to abuse Ecstasy than boys (65% versus 35%).

A warning concerning Ecstasy deserves mention here. Ecstasy, MDMA, is a powerful and selective poison to serotonergic fibers in the brain. While most studies in animal brains indicate these fibers can recover fully, the results in monkey brains indicate that a significant proportion (about 20%) never show normal recovery (Ricarurdi, McCann, Szabo, & Scheffel, 1997). Very long term deleterious effects on brain function have been documented in Ecstasy abusers (McCann, Merti, Eligulashvili, & Ricaurte, 1999). Thus, the users of Ecstasy should be forewarned of long term disruption to a key brain regulatory system, reduced cognitive functioning and emotional instability. This is especially important for teenage girls who use Ecstasy.

IMPACT OF AOD ABUSE DURING ADULTHOOD

After puberty, the brain slowly begins to age. Limbic structures, such as the hippocampus, significantly decrease in size by 35 years of age (Deleon et al., 1997). Neurotransmitters systems, like dopamine, are on the decline. Thus, the pleasure of certain drugs decreases because their biological targets are declining. Recreational substance use also decreases because of increased work and social demands. For example, it is difficult to take a major hallucinogen and be a responsible parent or worker. Despite this difficulty, many adults continue to abuse drugs. In many of these cases it can be argued they are trying to self-medicate a biologically imbalanced brain.

By the time most people reach adulthood, the brain has stopped expanding, and is beginning to show anatomical evidence of cortical shrinkage. It is harder to remember things, especially the names of people. This sense of impending doom can lead to the lure of quick fixes to improve brain functioning and self-medication with AOD. However, new evidence shows the adult brain, when properly nurtured, retains a great deal of neuroplasticity. Exercise, both mental and physical, shows evidence of invigorating brain function. Other helpful aids are a proper diet and approximately 8.2 hours of sleep a night.

If we accept that there are early predispositions to AOD abuse, then we can assume the brain has a chemical-structural imbalance. Drug usage may then be considered an attempt by the user to correct a brain-chemical imbalance, also known as "self-medication." For example, people who are depressed drink more and are more likely to become alcoholics. Treatment of this depression often alleviates the desire to drink (Kasper, Fuger, & Moller, 1992). Both anti-depressant medications and alcohol act on the Limbic System to counteract the depression. In addition, individuals suffering from anxiety are more likely to abuse marijuana. Marijuana, which is structurally similar to glucocorticoids steroids and has many receptors in the Limbic System, is believed to acutely reduce anxiety. Finally, individuals suffering from schizophrenia tend to be heavy cigarette smokers. Nicotine found in cigarettes induces a dose-dependent increase in neuronal activity due to its actions on the acetylcholinergic receptors (Stein et al., 1998). Nicotine has behavior-arousing and behavior-reinforcing properties in humans.

Self-medication has a paradoxical effect in that it may increase the symptoms that the person is seeking to relieve. For example, depressed patients who abuse alcohol and cocaine have increased, not reduced, suicidal ideation. They do not improve after typical antidepressant medication, but may actually get worse (Cornelius et al., 1998). Furthermore, the majority of adults who continue to chronically smoke marijuana do so because it helps them "relax" and better control the stressors of life. Yet prolonged marijuana use is associated with increased, not decreased, anxiety and aggression (Kouri, Pope, & Lucas, 1999). The same paradox is a hallmark of most drugs abused by adults, such as cocaine, heroine, depressants, and stimulants. *The more you take the drugs, the more likely you are to display the very symptoms you are trying to medicate.* And the brain systems and structures underlying these symptoms are also likely affected. As noted above, most people have a decrease in the uptake of dopamine as they age. Yet, individuals who abuse cocaine have a higher number of dopamine transporter binding sites on dopaminergic neurons, despite an apparent low number of total dopamine terminals. These abnormalities may contribute to the abnormalities in subjective experience and behavior characteristic of chronic cocaine abusers (Little et al., 1999). Thus, the intake of the drug finds more biological targets in a chronic user than would be present in a normal adult. It would appear that adults do not usually acquire an addiction, but maintain one started when they were young.

Why do adults continue to abuse a substance when they are aware it is harmful? Part of the answer may be that they lack the neural connections in the prefrontal cortex to comprehend this problem. Drugs can change brain connections in the very areas needed for higher order cognitive reasoning. The best illustration of this is found in alcoholics. Their brains are smaller. CAT scan studies show that the brains of 95% of the alcoholics and 67% of heavy social drinkers had decreased cortical volumes (Cala & Mastaglia, 1980). In particular, patients with a history of alcohol abuse show reductions in both the length and width of cortex (McShane & Willenbring, 1984). The frontal cortex is involved in evaluating and organizing actions. In alcoholics, this cortical region shows the greatest reductions in energy metabolism (Johnson-Greens, 1997). Thus, the brain region most needed to understand the consequence of the AOD abuse is the very region that is reduced.

However, animal studies have shown that while neurons are reduced in size, shape, and connectivity after chronic alcohol ingestion, the neurons are not killed. The cerebral cortex of rats given alcohol for two months showed a significant decrease in neuronal dendrites (Popova, 1996). When these animals stopped drinking alcohol for 40 days, there was a significant reversal in dendritic length back towards normal. The cells begin to assume their original size and establish neuronal connections. In a small clinical study done nearly 20 years ago, cerebral cortical volume and ventricle size was normal in nine alcoholics who practiced abstinence, compared to 15 subjects who were current alcoholics (Artmann, Gall, Hacker, & Herrlich, 1981). In a more recent study, the researchers found significant improvement within 16-30 days of abstinence (Volkow et al., 1994). A similar reversal of cortical loss is demonstrated in alcoholics with only a few months of abstinence (Carlen & Wilkinson, 1983). In a long-term study of 52 alcoholics, 72% had brain atrophy at the beginning of the study. In a five-year follow-up, the 16 subjects who had abstained from alcohol had significantly decreased cortical atrophy (Muuronen, Bergman, Hindmarsh, & Telakivi, 1989). The bottom line is that alcohol abuse results in a loss of cortical volume, not an increase in death of neurons, and this loss in volume may be reversed.

IMPACT OF AOD ABUSE DURING OLD AGE

Shakespeare had it right: The elderly are really in their second childhood. Just as the brains of children have immature neuronal connections and are in a period of rapid growth, so the brains of the elderly are losing connections and are in a period of rapid decline. While not all old people show evidence of cognitive loss, the incidence of dementia is greatly increased in individuals past the age of 70. The brain regions that are most vulnerable to the effects of aging are those of the Limbic System (the emotional centers). These areas, especially the hippocampus and temporal cortex, show the earliest sign of loss of volume in the brain associated with cognitive decline (DeLeon et al., 1997). It is not surprising that these same regions are most immature in the brains of children. *Thus the aged and the young have similar deficiencies in the emotional centers compared to normal adolescents and adults.*

The consequence of a limbic-compromised brain in the elderly leads to behavior that is reminiscent of the behavior of children, including emotional liability and difficulties dealing with complex issues. They are prone to accidents and often fail to consider the consequences of their actions. Their sleep is intermittent and easily disrupted. Since they have a compromised brain organization due to aging, elderly substance abusers are particularly vulnerable to become physically dependent. The abuse of drugs by this segment of the population is self-destructive in a very real sense (Eliason, 1998). The brain centers normally involved in addictive behavior (e.g., dopamine and serotonin) are dramatically reduced in the aged brain, so the positive-pleasure aspects of drug abuse are diminished. Hallucinogens and stimulants are not as appealing because the elderly have reduced cortical volume and are not seeking increased sensory stimulation. They lack a sense of experimentation and risk-behavior. The elderly are more likely to abuse alcohol and narcotics, drugs that deaden the senses to reality, not heighten them. Interestingly, a similar pattern is seen in young children. Unfortunately, the damaging effects of drugs are increased in the elderly. The kidney and liver are less efficient and more vulnerable to the toxic affects of alcohol and drugs. Neurons, normally showing age-related retraction of processes in an environment of reduced plasticity, are damaged by AOD abuse.

Alcohol is also a problem for the elderly, possibly for the same self-medication reasons as mentioned for adults. Many elderly are depressed, and although alcohol is effective at treating the symptoms of depression it also contributes to the underlying cause. Elderly patients who abuse alcohol and are depressed respond positively to antidepressant treatment (Oslin, Katz, & Edell, 2000). When the depressed elderly patients stopped drinking, even if it had been only in modest amounts, they showed even better improvement in mood. Much more attention is needed to these elderly people whose addiction is often invisible to society.

IMPLICATIONS FOR CLINICAL PRACTICE

Although tremendous progress has occurred in identifying trophic molecules and uncovering the biological pathways that support growth, much more research remains to be done. Drug abuse is a disease that can have a genetic predisposition. The search for the genes underlying drug addiction has received overwhelming support in the last decade. However, genetic research is not highly germane to the individual who must deal with environmental factors to fight addiction and associated risk behaviors. How can we make the brain of a child exposed prenatally to alcohol or cocaine stronger? What factors can be developed to deal with the complexity and surges of sex hormones in the brains of adolescents? Can adults be taught to give up reliance on an abused drug and seek alternative methods to satisfy their sense of imbalance? How can we reach the elderly and free them from the devastation of drugs on an aging brain? Attention to neuroplasticity and alcohol and drug abuse, including funding for education and research, needs to be increased.

Clinicians must recognize the biological affects of drug addiction and seek to reverse these affects by utilizing both biological and psychological manipulations (see article by Zweben in this volume). Solutions to the problem of AOD abuse may vary with individual cases. Will group or family therapy provide means to change brain connections? Can exercise, diet, sleep, light, vitamins or prescription drugs help an unbalanced brain achieve a normal homeostasis? Which are the best new medicines to prescribe? These questions need to be researched further. Clinicians and clients need education with regards to the impact of AOD on the brain so that they can have more realistic and scientifically sound expectations about the recovery process. This problem will most likely be resolved in a case-specific manner for each addict, through a collaborative effort made by an informed clinician, the patient, and family members.

CONCLUSION

The neurobiological consequences of AOD abuse have differential impacts during the five periods of life: perinatal, childhood, adolescence, adult and aged. The human brain changes throughout the life cycle–from the rapid growth phase in fetuses to the rapid decline in the elderly. Adolescents' neurons are exposed to major shifts in circulating steroids that promote growth of selective cells and alter brain connections. The adult brain, already in decline, shows an accelerated rate of reduction in volume due to alcohol and drug abuse. Dopamine neurons, considered the pleasure and addiction system, are more active at 18 years of age than at 80, so the pleasures of taking a drug which releases dopamine (e.g., cocaine, Ecstasy) should diminish as one ages. Drug and alcohol abuse should be considered in the context of these shifting patterns of brain growth.

The vulnerability of the brain to drugs and alcohol is a symptom of a biological predisposition, which can in some cases be attributed to "bad" genes, but is more likely attributed to the combined maturational (neurotrophic) actions of drugs, alcohol, and hormones (sex and stress). The brain becomes overly primed to receive sensory stimulation because of the growth of neuronal branches, which need increased activation. When these steroid systems are immature (as in children) or declining (as in the elderly), the neurons show a corresponding smaller morphology and a decrease in the urge to receive sensory stimulation. Knowledge of the capacity for neuroplasticity would be helpful in predicting treatment outcome.

A one-size-fits-all philosophy yearns for one gene, one drug, or one profession to provide the answer that will cure alcohol and drug addiction. There may be helpful hints, but addiction varies with age. Children and adults have different needs and mechanisms at work in the neuronal circuits. Alcohol and other drug addiction is a problem mankind has faced for thousands of years. The eventual solution will require a quantum evolutionary shift, implemented by social institutions endowed with biological insights into the neuroplasticity of the brain. The effective clinician will be a creative healer knowledgeable of the principles of neuroplasticity as they relate to human development and drug use.

NOTE

1. An analogy may help explain this concept. Suppose two people, who have never met, plan to meet at the airport in order to go on a trip together. If one of them is delayed, and the other waits at the airport, then they both miss the plane. They can still travel together but arrive later than expected as a pair. Alternatively, if one continues with their plans and leaves on the plane without the other, their trip will be completely independent of each other. Their failure to meet at the appointed time resulted in them never pairing up.

REFERENCES

Abraham, H. D., & Fava, M. (1999). Order of onset of substance abuse and depression in a sample of depressed outpatients. *Comprehensive Psychiatry*, *40*, 44-50.

Akbari, H. M., & Azmitia, E. C. (1992). Increased tyrosine hydroxylase immunoreactivity in the rat forebrain following prenatal cocaine exposure. *Developmental Brain Research*, *66*, 277-281.

Akbari, H. M., Whitaker-Azmitia, P. M., & Azmitia, E. C. (1994). Prenatal cocaine decreases the tropic factor S-100ß and induced microcephaly. *Neuroscience Letters*, *170*, 141-144.

Aramakis, V. B., Hsieh, C. Y., Leslie, F. M., & Metherate, R. (2000). A critical period for nicotine-induced disruption of synaptic development in rat auditory cortex. *Journal of Neuroscience*, *20* (16), 6106-6116.

Arendt, R., Angelopoulos, J., Salvator, A. & Singer, L. (1999). Motor development of cocaine-exposed children at age two years. *Pediatrics*, *103* (1), 86-92.

Artmann, H., Gall, M. V., Hacker, H., & Herrlich, J. (1981). Reversible enlargement of cerebral spinal fluid spaces in chronic alcoholics. *American Journal of Neuroradiology*, *2*, 23-27.

Azmitia, E. C. (1978). The serotonin producing neurons of the midbrain median and dorsal raphe nuclei. In L. L. Iversen, S. D. Iversen, & S. Snyder (Eds.), *The handbook of psychopharmacology* (Vol. 9, p. 233). New York: Plenum Press.

Azmitia, E. C., Liao, B., & Chen Y. (1993). Increase of tryptophan hydroxylase enzyme protein by dexamethasone in adrenalectomized rat midbrain. *Journal of Neuroscience*, *13* (12), 5041-5055.

Boyson, S. J., & Adams, C. E. (1997). D1 and D2 dopamine receptors in perinatal and adult basal ganglia. *Pediatric Research*, *41* (6), 822-831.

Cala, L. A., & Mastaglia, F. L. (1980). Computerized axial tomography in the detection of brain damage. 2. Epilepsy, migraine, and general medical disorders. *Medical Journal of Australia*, *29*, 616-620.

Carlen, P. L., & Wilkinson, D. A. (1983). Assessment of neurological dysfunction and recovery in alcoholics: CT scanning and other techniques. *Substance and Alcohol Actions/Misuse*, *4*, 191-197.

CASA (The National Center on Addiction and Substance Abuse at Columbia University) (1999). *The National Survey of American Attitudes on Substance Abuse: Teens and Their Parents* [On-line]. Available: http://www.casacolumbia.org/htm

Chiriboga, C. A., Brust, J. C., Bateman, D., & Hauser, W. A. (1999). Dose-response effect of fetal cocaine exposure on newborn neurologic function. *Pediatrics*, *103* (1), 79-85.

Cornelius, J. R., Salloum, I. M., Thase, M. E., Haskett, R. F., Daley, D. C., Jones-Barlock, A., Upsher, C., & Perel, J. M. (1998). Fluoxetine versus placebo in depressed alcoholic cocaine abusers. *Psychopharmacology Bulletin*, *34* (1), 117-121.

De Leon, M. J., George, A. E., Golomb, J., Tarshish, C., Convit, A., Kluger, A., De Santi, S., McRae, T., Ferris, S. H., Reisberg, B., Ince, C., Rusinek, H., Bobinski, M., Quinn, B., Miller, D. C., & Wisniewski, H. M. (1997). Frequency of hippocampal formation atrophy in normal aging and Alzheimer's disease. *Neurobiology of Aging*, *18*, 1-11.

Dempsey, D., Jacob, P. 3rd, Partridge, J. C., Jones, R.T., Panganiban, K., & Rowbotham, M. C. (1999). Cocaine metabolite kinetics in the newborn. *Journal of Analytical Toxicology*, *24*, 8-15.

DuRant, R. H., & Simmons, J. M. (1999). Perceived adult disapproval of substance use, disapproval of peer substance use, family factors and frequency of alcohol and marijuana use by adolescents. *Journal of Adolescent Health*, *24* (2), 129.

Eliason, M. J. (1998). Identification of alcohol-related problems in older women. *Journal of Gerontological Nursing*, *24* (10), 8-15.

Garcia-Segura, L. M., Chowen, J. A., Parducz, A., & Naftolin, F. (1994). Gonadal hormones as promoters of structural synaptic plasticity: Cellular mechanisms. *Progress in Neurobiology, 44*, 279-307.

Harding, A. J., Wong, A., Svoboda, M., Kril, J. J., & Halliday, G. M. (1997). Chronic alcohol consumption does not cause hippocampal neuron loss in humans. *Hippocampus, 7* (1), 78-87.

Harwell, T. S., Spence, M. R., Sands, A., & Iguchi, M. Y. (1996). Substance use in an inner-city family planning population. *Journal of Reproductive Medicine, 41*, 704-710.

Hellstrom-Lindahl, E., & Court, J. A. (2000). Nicotinic acetylcholine receptors during prenatal development and brain pathology in human aging. *Behavioral Brain Research, 113*, 159-168.

Henderson, S. (1993). Women, sexuality and ecstasy use–The Final Report, Lifeline, Manchester, England.

Johnson-Greene, D., Adams, K. M., Gilman, S., Koeppe, R. A., Junck, L., Kluin, K. J., Martorello, S., & Heumann, M. (1997). Effects of abstinence and relapse upon neuropsychological function and cerebral glucose metabolism in severe chronic alcoholism. *Journal of Clinical & Experimental Neuropsychology, 19*, 378-385.

Kafka, M. P., & Prentky, R. A. (1998). Attention-deficit/hyperactivity disorder in males with paraphilias and paraphilia-related disorders: A comorbidity study. *Journal of Clinical Psychiatry, 59*, 388-395.

Karlix, J. L., Behnke, M., Davis-Eyler, F., Wobie, K., Adams, V., Freiburger, B., Conlon, M., & Tebbett, I. R. (1998). Cocaine suppresses fetal immune system. *Pediatric Research, 44* (1), 43-46.

Kasper, S., Fuger, J., & Moller, H. J. (1992). Comparative efficacy of antidepressants. *Drugs, 43*, (Supplement 2), 11-22.

Korbo, L. (1999). Glial cell loss in the hippocampus of alcoholics. *Alcoholism: Clinical and Experimental Research, 23* (1), 164-168.

Kouri, E. M., Pope, H. G. Jr., & Lukas, S. E. (1999). Changes in aggressive behavior during withdrawal from long-term marijuana use. *Psychopharmacology, 143* (3), 302-308.

Little, K. Y., Zhang, L., Desmond, T., Frey, K. A., Dalack, G. W., & Cassin, B. J. (1999). Striatal dopaminergic abnormalities in human cocaine users. *American Journal of Psychiatry, 156* (2), 238-245.

Long, J. M., Mouton, P. R., Jucker, M., & Ingram, D. K. (1999). What counts in brain aging? Design-based stereological analysis of cell number. *Journal of Gerontology. Series A. Biological Science and Medical Science, 54*, B407-417.

McCann, U. D., Mertl, M., Eligulashvili, V., & Ricaurte, G. A. (1999). Cognitive performance in (+/−) 3,4-methylenedioxymethamphetamine (MDMA, "ecstasy") users: A controlled study. *Psychopharmacology, 143* (4), 417-425.

McShane, D., & Willenbring, M. L. (1984). Differences in cerebral asymmetries related to drinking history and ethnicity: A computerized axial tomography (CAT) scan study. *Journal of Nervous and Mental Disease, 172* (9), 529-532.

Msall, M. E., Bier, J. A., LaGasse, L., Tremont, M., & Lester, B. (1998). The vulnerable preschool child: The impact of biomedical and social risks on neurodevelopmental function. *Seminars in Pediatric Neurology, 5*, 52-61.

Muuronen, A., Bergman, H., Hindmarsh, T., & Telakivi, T. (1998). Influence of improved drinking habits on brain atrophy and cognitive performance in alcoholic patients: A 5-year follow-up study. *Alcoholism: Clinical and Experimental Research, 13* (1), 137-141.

Ness, R. B., Grisso, J. A., Hirschinger, N., Markovic, N., Shaw, L. M., Day, N. L., & Kline, J. (1999). Cocaine and tobacco use and the risk of spontaneous abortion. *The New England Journal of Medicine, 340* (5), 333-339.

Novins, D. K., & Mitchell, C. M. (1998). Factors associated with marijuana use among American Indian adolescents. *Addiction, 93,* 1693-1702.

Oslin, D. W., Katz, I. R., Edell, W. S., Ten, H., & Thomas, R. (2000). Effects of alcohol consumption on the treatment of depression among elderly patients. *American Journal of Geriatric Psychiatry, 8,* 215-220.

Popova, E. N. (1999). Changes in cortical neurons and their dendrites after chronic alcoholic intoxication. *Bulleten Eksperimentalnoi Biologii I Meditsiny, 122,* 467-470.

Proimos, J., DuRant, R. H., Pierce, J. D., & Goodman, E. (1998). Gambling and other risk behaviors among 8th- to 12th-grade students. *Pediatrics, 102,* e23.

Ricaurte, G. A., McCann, U. D., Szabo, Z., & Scheffel, U. (2000). Toxicodynamics and long-term toxicity of the recreational drug, 3, 4-methylenedioxymethamphetamine (MDMA, 'Ecstasy'). *Toxicology Letters, 112-113,* 143-146.

Richardson, G. A. (1998). Prenatal cocaine exposure: A longitudinal study of development. *Annals of the New York Academy of Sciences, 846,* 144-152.

Roy, T. S., & Sabherwal, U. (1994). Effects of prenatal nicotine exposure on the morphogenesis of somatosensory cortex. *Neurotoxicology and Teratology, 16* (4), 411-421.

Sanchez-Martin, J. R., Fano, E., Ahedo, L., Cardas, J., Brain, P. F., & Azpiroz, A. (2000). Relating testosterone levels and free play social behavior in male and female preschool children. *Psychoneuroendocrinology, 25,* 773-783.

Schootman, M., Fuortes, L. J., Zwerling, C., Albanese, M. A., & Watson, C. A. (1993). Safety behavior among Iowa junior high and high school students. *American Journal of Public Health, 83* (11), 1628-1630.

Smythe, J. W., Rowe, W. B., & Meaney, M. J. (1994). Neonatal handling alters serotonin (5-HT) turnover and 5-HT-Sub-2 receptor binding in selected brain regions: Relationship to the handling effect on glucocorticoid receptor expression. *Brain Research. Developmental Brain Research, 80* (1-2), 183-189.

Soyibo, K., & Lee, M. G. (1999). Use of illicit drugs among high-school students in Jamaica. *Bulletin of the World Health Organization, 77,* 258-262.

Stanger, C., Higgins, S. T., Bickel, W. K., Elk, R., Grabowski, J., Schmitz, J., Amass, L., Kirby, K. C., & Seracini, A. M. (1999). Behavioral and emotional problems among children of cocaine- and opiate-dependent parents. *Journal of the American Academy of Child & Adolescent Psychiatry, 38,* 421-428.

Stein, E. A., Pankiewicz, J., Harsch, H. H., Cho, J. K., Fuller, S. A., Hoffmann, R. G., Hawkins, M., Rao, S. M., Bandettini, P. A., & Bloom, A. S. (1998). Nicotine-induced limbic cortical activation in the human brain: A functional MRI study. *American Journal of Psychiatry, 155* (8), 1009-1015.

Tajuddin, N. F., & Druse, M. J. (1999). In utero ethanol exposure decreased the density of serotonin neurons. Maternal ipsapirone treatment exerted a protective effect. *Brain Research. Developmental Brain Research, 117* (1), 91-97.

Taylor, D., Estevez, V.S., Englert, L. F., & Ho, B. T. (1976). Hydrolysis of carbon labeled cocaine in human serum. *Research Communications in Chemical Pathology & Pharmacology, 14*, 249-257.

Vega, W. A., Alderete, E., Kolody, B., & Aguilar-Gaxiola, S. (1998). Illicit drug use among Mexicans and Mexican Americans in California: The effects of gender and acculturation. *Addiction, 93*, 1839-1850.

Volkow, N. D., Fowler, J. S., Wolf, A. P., Hitzemann, R., Dewey, S., Bendriem, B., Alpert, R., & Hoff, A. (1991). Changes in brain glucose metabolism in cocaine dependence and withdrawal. *American Journal of Psychiatry, 148* (5), 621-626.

Weissman, M. M., Warner, V., Wickramaratne, P. J., & Kandel, D. B. (1999). Maternal smoking during pregnancy and psychopathology in offspring followed to adulthood. *Journal of the American Academy of Child & Adolescent Psychiatry, 38*, 892-899.

Zahalka, E. A., Seidler, F. J., Lappi, S. E., McCook, E. C., Yanai, J., & Slotkin, T. A. (1992). Deficits in development of central cholinergic pathways caused by fetal nicotine exposure: Differential effects on choline acetyltransferase activity and [3H]hemicholinium-3 binding. *Neurotoxicology and Teratology, 14* (6), 375-382.

Zuckerman, B., Frank, D. A., Hingson, R., Amaro, H., Levenson, S. M., Kayne, H., Parker, S., Vinci, R., Aboagye, K., Fried, L. E. et al. (1998). Effects of maternal marijuana and cocaine use on fetal growth. *The New England Journal of Medicine, 320* (12), 762-768.

Integrating Pharmacotherapy and Psychosocial Interventions in the Treatment of Individuals with Alcohol Problems

Allen Zweben

SUMMARY. Both research and clinical experiences suggest that there are separate and overlapping benefits of medications and psychosocial treatments for alcohol problems. Evidence has shown that medication(s) combined with a moderate intensity psychosocial therapy can produce outcomes beyond what each of these approaches can produce alone. Taking medication can be helpful in facilitating longer periods of abstinence that in turn affords practitioners a greater opportunity to enhance patients' individual and social coping resources and to increase their motivation to change. Combining effective pharmacological and psychosocial interventions may provide the impetus to integrate alcoholism treatment into the general health care delivery system, thereby helping to increase the accessibility of care and well-being for individuals seeking or needing help with alcohol problems. *[Article copies available for a fee from The Haworth Document Delivery Service: 1-800-342-9678. E-mail address: <getinfo@haworthpressinc.com> Website: <http://www.HaworthPress.com> © 2001 by The Haworth Press, Inc. All rights reserved.]*

Allen Zweben, DSW, is Professor and Director, Center for Addiction and Behavioral Health Research, School of Social Welfare, University of Wisconsin-Milwaukee, P.O. Box 786, Milwaukee, WI 53201.

[Haworth co-indexing entry note]: "Integrating Pharmacotherapy and Psychosocial Interventions in the Treatment of Individuals with Alcohol Problems." Zweben, Allen. Co-published simultaneously in *Journal of Social Work Practice in the Addictions* (The Haworth Social Work Practice Press, an imprint of The Haworth Press, Inc.) Vol. 1, No. 3, 2001, pp. 65-80; and: *Neurobiology of Addictions: Implications for Clinical Practice* (ed: Richard T. Spence, Diana M. DiNitto, and Shulamith Lala Ashenberg Straussner) The Haworth Social Work Practice Press, an imprint of The Haworth Press, Inc., 2001, pp. 65-80. Single or multiple copies of this article are available for a fee from The Haworth Document Delivery Service [1-800-342-9678, 9:00 a.m. - 5:00 p.m. (EST). E-mail address: getinfo@ haworthpressinc.com].

KEYWORDS. Pharmacotherapy, psychosocial therapy, alcoholism treatment outcomes, clinical trials, health care delivery

Recent developments in pharmacotherapy and psychosocial interventions have provided the impetus for combining these interventions for improving treatment outcomes for large numbers of patients currently seen in clinical settings. Evidence has shown that combining psychosocial and pharmacotherapy interventions can produce outcomes beyond what each of the aforementioned approaches can produce alone. Medications can help to sustain a longer period of abstinence that in turn can help to enhance individuals' social coping resources and increase their motivation to change. This paper will examine the rationale and evidence for combining pharmacotherapy and psychosocial interventions and discuss how such an integrated approach may help to improve the alcohol treatment delivery system.

IMPORTANT ADVANCES IN PHARMACOLOGIC AGENTS FOR THE TREATMENT OF ALCOHOL PROBLEMS

Within the past eight years, the National Institute of Alcohol Abuse and Alcoholism (NIAAA) has supported several studies involving the use of medications for the treatment of alcohol problems (Litten, Fertig, & Allen, 1999). One such medication is naltrexone, a long-acting opioid antagonist that reduces craving resulting from the reinforcing effects of alcohol. The benefits of naltrexone on abstinence have been linked with a sustained period of abstinence and in preventing a slip or "set-back" from turning into a "full-blown" relapse. In one study (O'Malley et al., 1992), naltrexone was found to be superior to placebo in increasing abstinent days when combined with either coping skills or supportive therapy. In the same study, the likelihood of returning to heavy drinking following an initial drink was less for patients receiving 50 mg of naltrexone daily than for placebo treated patients (O'Malley et al., 1996). However these benefits were evident only for four months following the 12 weeks of active treatment (O'Malley et al., 1996). This raises an important question about the medication, namely, how to extend the benefits of naltrexone so that longer periods of abstinence are achieved or at least how to further delay relapse.

Another promising medication, acamprosate, a glutamate antagonistic, addresses the negative effects of protracted withdrawal. Acamprosate has been shown to be effective in a multicenter, randomized control trial conducted in Europe. This large scale trial (more than 4,000 patients) combined acamprosate with routine psychosocial treatment (cf. Aubin, 1996; Sass et al., 1996; Soyka, 1996). Ten of the eleven treatment centers in the trial demonstrated superior results of acamprosate compared with the control group (Soyka, 1995). More specifically, acamprosate patients had a total abstinence rate of 43% compared to 21% for placebo patients (Sass et al., 1996), a 2-to-1 abstinence rate. Similar results were found in the U.S. multisite acamprosate trial. The acamprosate group had 70% abstinence days vs. 58% abstinence days for the placebo group. However, enthusiasm for these findings is dampened somewhat by the following limitations: high attrition rates (i.e., 60-70% of the acamprosate patients terminated treatment prematurely in the European study); the lack of standardized criteria for diagnosing alcoholism in the European study; and the failure to standardize and specify the psychosocial treatment in the European study or monitor the psychosocial treatment in the U.S. study.

Without standardizing and fully specifying and monitoring the psychosocial treatment, it is difficult to articulate the content and intensity of the behavioral treatment that should be offered in conjunction with the medication. To illustrate, there were significantly fewer depressive episodes when geriatric patients were given the antidepressant medication nortriptyline *and* interpersonal therapy, than when receiving nortriptyline *alone* (Reynolds et al., 1999). In this rigorously designed study, the investigators employed a well-specified, standardized, manual-driven psychotherapy targeted at treating depressive disorders in order to answer the question of what kind of psychosocial treatment should accompany the medication to produce the optimal benefits for the target population.

PROMISING PSYCHOSOCIAL TREATMENTS FOR ALCOHOL PROBLEMS

There is now strong evidence that a brief or moderate intensity intervention is as effective or more effective than more intensive or conventional strategies in addressing alcohol problems. One such approach is brief motivational treatment (BMT). This intervention attempts to improve drinking outcomes by employing strategies aimed at rapidly enhancing motivational readiness, self-efficacy, and compliance in an alcohol dependent population. Project MATCH, a multisite, collaborative trial, found that a brief motivational treatment, termed Motivational Enhancement Therapy (MET), did not differ significantly from a more intensive cognitive behavioral therapy (CBT) or a more traditional twelve-step facilitation approach (TSF) in treating alcohol problems (Project MATCH Research Group, 1997). All three approaches produced significant pre-post improvement in drinking behavior and related issues (e.g., social functioning and emotional problems). While TSF and CBT treatments yielded slightly greater (two more abstinent days per month) reduction in drinking, post-treatment follow-up drinking rates did not differ significantly among the three treatment groups (Project MATCH Research Group, 1998). In addition, there was no differential in total health care costs associated with MET, CBT, and TSF (Holder et al., 2000). The mean estimated monthly post-treatment costs for the three treatment conditions ranged from $359 for MET to a high of $433 for CBT and $407 for TSF (Holder et al., 2000). However, MET had a clear cost advantage over CBT and TSF since it was less expensive treatment to deliver (Cisler et al., 1999).

Cognitive behavioral therapy (CBT) is another promising approach for treating alcohol problems. Based upon social learning theory, CBT focuses on the learning of alternative coping strategies rather than drinking. Opportunities are provided to build confidence and develop practice skills focused on enhancing assertiveness, controlling anger, managing moods, and improving communication. CBT has demonstrated efficacy when it was delivered as part of a comprehensive treatment program rather than as a stand-alone approach. In reviewing the outcome literature on CBT, Longabaugh and Morgenstern (1999) found that CBT was more effective than other treatments (e.g., interactional therapy) within programs targeted at changing an individual's social environment. The latter involved creating an alternative lifestyle that would be incompatible with drinking (i.e., avoiding "drinking buddies," finding regular employment, attending church services, etc.). Similar results occurred when CBT was added to pharmacotherapy and when it was compared with other approaches (e.g., brief supportive counseling) also delivered in conjunction with the medication (Litten, Fertig, & Allen, 1999).

Relationship enhancement therapies (RETs) have found increasing support in the alcoholism treatment outcome literature. RETs involve a variety of different but related approaches all aimed at increasing social support for abstinence, buttressing motivation, improving interaction patterns that promote and reinforce sobriety, and establishing and maintaining emotional ties with members of the social network. Although there are conceptual differences among these approaches (e.g., a basis in systems theory vs. social learning theory), all involve the promotion and active involvement of a significant other (SO), whether it is a spouse, child, relative, friend, or member of a self-help group, in facilitating change in the alcohol dependent patient. RETs include: Significant other-involved brief treatment (Zweben & Barrett, 1993), behavioral marital or family therapy (O'Farrell, 1995; Miller et al., 1999), and mutual help (e.g., AA Fellowship) (Emrick et al., 1993; Tonigan & Toscova, 1998) or twelve-step facilitation (TSF), an approach that encourages or supports AA attendance and involvement (Project MATCH Research Group, 1997).

Long-term outcomes demonstrate the advantages of RET over individual-focused alcohol therapies in terms of improving interpersonal relationships and sustaining sobriety (O'Farrell & Fals-Stewart, 1999). Evidence shows that RETs are particularly valuable in facilitating medication and treatment compliance (O'Farrell, 1995; Sisson & Azrin, 1986; Zweben, Pearlman, & Li, 1983; Miller et al., 1999). RET has demonstrated effectiveness in helping individuals to enter and remain in treatment even if the individual is unwilling to make the initial treatment contact him/herself (Zweben, Pearlman, & Li, 1983; Miller et al., 1999).

In Project MATCH, individuals whose pretreatment environments were highly supportive of drinking fared better when assigned to twelve-step facilitation (TSF) than motivational enhancement therapy (MET). This finding was attributed to TSF's mutual support and encouragement of patients to attend AA. At the three-year follow-up, among patients whose social environments were highly supportive of drinking, the TSF group had 16% more abstinent days (74% vs. 58%) than the MET group (Longabaugh et al., 1998).

Westerberg (1998), in reviewing the alcoholism literature on relapse, concluded that individuals who are able to maintain the positive gains of treatment are typically those who have strong social support for abstinence. One inference that can be drawn from these findings is that consideration should be given to adding RET to all forms of psychosocial counseling, whether it is in the form of having a supportive significant other (SSO) participate in the sessions, encouraging attendance at mutual help groups, or both.

RATIONALE FOR COMBINING PHARMACOTHERAPY AND PSYCHOSOCIAL THERAPY FOR ALCOHOL PROBLEMS

There is reason to believe that integrating pharmacotherapy and psychosocial therapy can have a potentiating effect on alcohol patients (Carroll, 1997). This means that together the two interventions (medication and psychosocial intervention) might be more effective in treating alcohol problems than either one of the approaches employed separately. Figure 1 shows the proposed separate and overlapping benefits of medication and psychosocial treatments. The figure illustrates that there is a synergistic relationship between psychosocial and medication approaches.

Both clinical experience and research remind us of the benefits gained in employing a combined approach for treating alcohol problems. Behavioral intervention interacts with or complements pharmacological interventions in the following ways:

1. Individuals' beliefs about their drinking problem could undermine their adherence to the medication regime. They may be less willing to tolerate early side effects of the medication if they believe that the drinking problem is "not that serious" or if they believe that the drinking problem is a psychological or moral issue that is not responsive to medication.

2. Some individuals may be unable to employ coping methods for everyday living without achieving a sustained period of abstinence. For some patients, a period of sustained abstinence can only be achieved if they take the medication regularly to manage the unpleasant effects of craving.

3. Merely advising patients about the positive "track record" of the medication will not ensure medication compliance or positive outcomes. There is a host of individual, interactional, and contextual factors that could sabotage pharmacological treatment. For example, a practitioner's inability to connect with the client may contribute to mistrust and misunderstandings about the medication.

4. Patients may have unstable relationships and sundry concrete problems in their daily lives that could interfere with following a medication regime.

5. Not sufficiently attending to the physical aspects of the medication, i.e., a patient's discomfort in taking the pills could undermine the working alliance established between practitioner and patient.

6. A change in drinking behavior resulting from the medication could engender other problems in the household. The non-drinking partner may be reluctant to share decision-making responsibilities or reengage in a sexual relationship even though the patient has achieved abstinence. Rather than attend to the marital conflict, the patient may decide to stop taking the medication and resume drinking.

These experiences illustrate how medications and psychosocial interventions help to support change efforts of patients. Taking medication allows the cells in the brain to readapt to a normal (nonalcoholic) state, thereby enabling patients to think more clearly and have more positive emotional responses, which in turn may strengthen coping resources, enhance self-esteem, and in general, increase motivational readiness to change.

My own experiences in conducting pharmacotherapy trials might help to shed further light on this issue. I have found that the availability of new medications has enabled us to recruit individuals into treatment who identify themselves as "failures" in traditional alcohol programs or are reluctant to participate in programs that primarily involve "talk" therapy. For these individuals, receiving medication along with psychosocial therapy appears to help destigmatize the drinking problem while increasing their optimism about change.

FIGURE 1. Proposed Benefits of Psychosocial Treatment and Medication

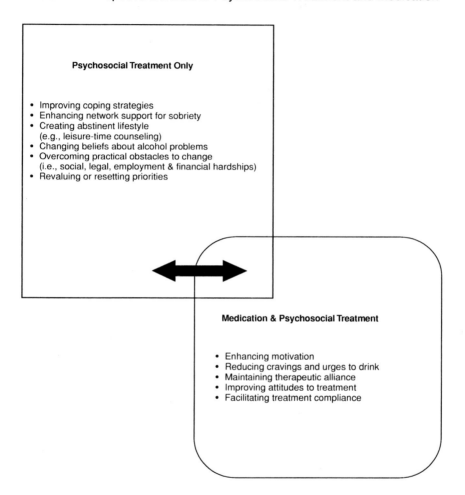

Psychosocial Treatment Only

- Improving coping strategies
- Enhancing network support for sobriety
- Creating abstinent lifestyle
  (e.g., leisure-time counseling)
- Changing beliefs about alcohol problems
- Overcoming practical obstacles to change
  (i.e., social, legal, employment & financial hardships)
- Revaluing or resetting priorities

Medication & Psychosocial Treatment

- Enhancing motivation
- Reducing cravings and urges to drink
- Maintaining therapeutic alliance
- Improving attitudes to treatment
- Facilitating treatment compliance

RESEARCH SUPPORT FOR INTEGRATING MEDICATIONS AND PSYCHOSOCIAL TREATMENT TO IMPROVE COMPLIANCE AND TREATMENT OUTCOMES

Employing motivational strategies targeted at medication adherence issues has been found useful in decreasing ambivalence or modifying expectations about the alcohol medication, resulting in better medication adherence outcomes (Pettinati et al., 2000). There is evidence demonstrating that response to medication is highly dependent upon producing an adherence effect (Volpicelli et al., 1997). For example, Volpicelli et al. (1997) observed significant differences between naltrexone and placebo subjects *only* among compliant subjects (i.e., individuals taking the medication or placebo on 90% or more of the study days). Medication adherent subjects were abstinent on 98% of the study days as compared with 89% for placebo subjects. In contrast, among individuals with lower medication adherence (i.e., taking the medication or placebo < 90% of study days), no significant differences were observed between naltrexone and placebo subjects on drinking measures. These results replicate an earlier finding dealing with medication adherence (Volpicelli et al., 1992).

In addition, the type of therapy received along with the medication appears to make a difference with regard to treatment outcomes. In an innovative study, O'Malley (reported in Litten, Fertig, & Allen, 1999) randomized "treatment responders" to either of the following conditions over a six-month period: (1) continued administration of the study medication (naltrexone) or (2) placebo. "Treatment responders" were identified in an earlier trial as those who had no more than two days of heavy drinking in the last four weeks and took naltrexone at least 60% of the time. In this continuation study, among subjects who received primary care counseling (brief advice and support) in the earlier study, those placed on placebo drank more often and had more heavy drinking days than did naltrexone-treated subjects. However, interestingly, subjects receiving CBT in the earlier study were able to maintain treatment gains throughout the six month period regardless of whether they were assigned to a placebo or naltrexone condition. One inference that can be made here is that CBT could produce outcomes beyond what the medication might produce with a less intensive form of therapy such as brief advice and support.

These studies raise important questions for future research. One question is to determine the relative efficacy of more intensive behavioral treatment versus less intensive treatment with and without the presence of active medications. Another issue is to compare different behavioral modalities with the presence of active medication, with placebo, or without pills at all. To answer such questions, a request for proposals on this topic was circulated by NIAAA in 1997, and eleven sites located in different geographic regions were selected to participate in this multi-site collaborative project, which was eventually termed the COMBINE Study. The Center for Addiction and Behavioral Health Research (CABHR) in the School of Social Welfare, University of Wisconsin-Milwaukee was selected as one of the participating sites with the author (AZ) as the principal investigator of the Wisconsin site.

THE COMBINE STUDY–AN ILLUSTRATION

The COMBINE study is an NIAAA-funded, six-year research project investigating the efficacy of combining medications and psychotherapy for the treatment of alcohol problems. COMBINE is evaluating the efficacy of promising medications, naltrexone and acamprosate (discussed earlier), and two forms of behavioral treatments individually and in combination. In general, research questions are focused on whether more intensive interventions such as combining medications (i.e., acamprosate and naltrexone) and a moderate intensity behavioral intervention produce better outcomes than less intervention approaches (e.g., placebo and minimal intervention). The overall hypothesis is that combining the two medications with a moderate intensity behavioral treatment will yield better outcomes for alcohol dependent patients.

Treatment Approaches

Combined Behavioral Intervention (CBI). The COMBINE study has developed an innovative treatment approach termed combined behavioral intervention (CBI). CBI incorporates several elements of promising treatment approaches (mentioned earlier), namely, brief motivational counseling, cognitive behavioral treatment, and relationship enhancement therapy. CBI integrates various elements of these therapies found to be effective in addressing the special needs and capacities of dependent drinkers. CBI involves: (1) sundry motivational strategies to address different levels of motivational readiness found in patients, (2) coping skills training to address deficit areas such as poor communication, high anger, and other life problems, and (3) a relationship enhancement approach in the form of having a supportive significant other (SSO) attend and participate in the treatment sessions and/or encouraging participation in mutual help groups, particularly for those lacking ongoing social support for sobriety. All these components of CBI have been tested in prior studies and shown to have reasonable evidence of efficacy for the treatment of alcohol problems. For example, motivational strategies have been found to be as, or more, effective than conventional approaches in at least 16 controlled trials in terms of improving compliance and treatment outcome (Bien et al., 1993). A comprehensive coping skills training approach (including a functional analysis) has demonstrated efficacy in a variety of alcohol treatment outcome studies (Miller, 1998). And finally, SSO involvement and mutual help seem to be valuable adjuncts to alcoholism treatment by mobilizing or supporting an individual's attempts in achieving and maintaining abstinence. In Project MATCH, better outcomes were obtained among patients who had an SSO attend at least one treatment session. However, the presence of an SSO was noted in a minority of cases in Project MATCH. SSO involvement was more often found in MET (18% of the cases involved an SSO) than in the other two MATCH treatments. It has been speculated that greater emphasis may have been given to SSO involvement in MET than the other therapies.

In addition, unlike prior treatment outcome research, session attendance is flexible based on individual needs, capacities, resources, and desires/expectations of patients. CBI's functional analysis assists practitioners in determining which treatment components or modules might be most suitable for the patient's problems. A decision to include certain modules (such as communication training) is based on evidence of their efficacy in addressing the patient's particular problem. In accordance with a motivational style approach, the following procedures are employed: (1) patients are provided with a menu of options targeted to specific problems or issues; (2) they are informed of how a particular option might be employed to address their alcohol-related problems; and (3) they are asked to consider which issues they are most committed to working on during the course of the study treatment period. A treatment plan is eventually devised based on the results of this process. Patients are allowed up to 20 sessions delivered over the 16-week treatment period.

For further clarification, the four phases of CBI are outlined in Table 1. Phases one and two usually occur in the first four weeks of treatment. The foci of these phases are: (1) establishing a therapeutic relationship, (2) eliciting and clarifying the patient's concerns about the drinking and related life problems, and (3) enhancing intrinsic motivation to change. Feedback from the pretreatment assessment is presented with the aim of identifying issues or problems associated with drinking, devising a tentative treatment plan, and obtaining a commitment to carry out the proposed plan. Evaluating and enlisting the involvement of the SSO typically occurs in these initial phases. Phase three involves the implementation of treatment modules negotiated in phase two. There are 16 modules to choose from in phase three including: mood management, assertiveness training, communication skills training, job finding skills, and leisure-time planning. Phase four entails evaluating whether goals are maintained and modifying treatment plans if necessary. Also, this phase is aimed at renewing or bolstering motivation and preparing the patient for termination. Phases three and four may take up to 16 sessions.

Medical Management. CBI is compared with medical management (MM), a less intensive intervention derived from what has been generically termed "brief intervention" (Heather, 1995). MM is aimed at facilitating medication compliance and support for sobriety and can be employed opportunistically in primary care or health care settings where alcohol dependent patients may be seen. MM is considered a cost-effective alternative to CBI and can be more

TABLE 1. Four Phases of CBI

Phase one	Enhancing commitment to change
Phase two	Developing a treatment plan
Phase three	Implementing selected treatment modules
Phase four	Maintaining and monitoring treatment plans

easily employed than the latter since less training or experience is required for practitioners conducting the intervention.

Many of the components of brief intervention, such as giving advice on how to remain abstinent and encouraging involvement in mutual self-help groups (e.g., AA), have been adopted in MM. Much emphasis is placed on addressing medication compliance issues related to side effects, negative attitudes toward pill-taking, and logistical problems (i.e., following the dosage schedule). For practical purposes, MM sessions are limited to 15-25 minutes in duration (except for the initial MM visit which requires a physical examination). This means that MM strategies could be mastered with limited training and delivered within a typical visit to a physician or nurse practitioner in a busy medical setting. All together, MM is delivered nine times over the 16-week treatment period.

Study Design

The COMBINE study employs an additive design to test whether CBI + MM with and without the presence of naltrexone and/or acamprosate is more effective than MM with and without the presence of these medications. Table 2 describes the design of the study.

Patients are randomized to one of nine pharmacological and psychosocial treatment combinations. The ninth cell is included to test the incremental efficacy of providing pills along with CBI. This enables us to determine whether the effects of the psychosocial therapy are the same regardless of whether pills (i.e., active medication or placebo) are administered to patients. Further analysis involves (1) comparing the treatment effects of naltrexone vs. acamprosate (cell 2 vs. cell 3) and naltrexone + acamprosate vs. naltrexone or acamprosate delivered alone (cell 4 vs. cells 2 or 3), (2) comparing the treatment effects of MM + CBI (cell 5) vs. MM delivered alone (i.e., with placebo) (cell 1), and comparing the treatment effects of both combining the study medications (i.e., naltrexone and acamprosate) and the behavioral treatments (i.e., MM + CBI) (cell 8) vs. combining the study medications with MM alone (cell 4). Such an analysis allows us to evaluate the intensity and context of psychosocial treat-

TABLE 2. COMBINE Study Design

		Psychosocial Treatment Condition		
		Medical Management	Medical Management + Combined Behavioral Intervention	Combined Behavioral Intervention
Medication Condition	Placebo	1	5	
	Naltrexone	2	6	
	Acamprosate	3	7	
	Naltrexone + Acamprosate	4	8	
	No Pills			9

ment. Because the study is being conducted in primary care clinics and specialized settings, these findings are applicable to both types of settings.

The study involves 1,375 alcohol dependent patients. Each patient receives four months of treatment and is requested to participate in 12 months of follow-up. The primary drinking outcome measures are percent days abstinent and time to relapse to heavy drinking. A variety of assessment domains are included dealing with medical tests, motivation, social support, self-efficacy, alcohol-related consequences (e.g., marital conflict), psychological functioning, psychiatric symptomatology, medical care costs, and health utilization, quality of life, and treatment compliance.

CONCLUSIONS

Recent research has shown that a combination of promising psychosocial interventions and pharmacotherapies offers an attractive alternative to current approaches for treating alcohol dependent patients. The proposed combinations have the potential to increase abstinence rates for those patients typically seen in alcohol treatment programs. For example, in Project MATCH, despite substantial improvement rates among outpatients in terms of increasing the frequency of abstinent days, only 20% of these outpatients were able to remain completely abstinent through the 12-month follow-up period. Thus, medications such as acamprosate and naltrexone have the potential for reducing the unpleasant effects of craving during the first three months of treatment–a particularly vulnerable period for alcohol dependent patients, culminating in a sustained period of abstinence. This can help practitioners work more successfully at increasing motivational readiness, enhancing self-efficacy, and mobilizing appropriate individual and social coping resources.

Social work practitioners need to gain familiarity with these new medications along with the state-of-the-art techniques on motivational interviewing, cognitive behavioral treatment, and relationship enhancement therapies to better serve their alcohol dependent patients. Knowledge of these pharmacological and psychosocial methods should be integrated in the curriculum offered by schools of social work along with recent evidence demonstrating their utility with alcohol dependent patients. In line with the latter objective, the National Institute on Alcohol Abuse and Alcoholism (NIAAA) has recently formed an expert panel to develop an up-to-date social work curriculum for the prevention and treatment of alcohol use disorders. Modules on medications and psychosocial interventions for alcohol problems along with information on screening and assessment, epidemiology, alcohol treatment delivery system, and ethical issues will be incorporated into the new curriculum.

Future research will need to go beyond testing whether combinations of drugs and psychosocial therapies produce better outcomes. Researchers will need to examine the mechanisms of action related to the drugs and psychosocial therapies that might account for the behavioral change. For example, we need to know which drugs interfere with the reinforcement effects of drinking, which drugs reverse the negative effects of prolonged withdrawal, and which of the different neurotransmitter systems are involved in the process. We need to know more about which components of the psychosocial interventions (e.g., certain elements of skill training vs. specific motivational interviewing techniques) are most salient in producing change in terms of drinking and related problems. Also, how should practitioners deliver these psychosocial interventions and medications (e.g., dosages and sequencing) to maximize change in different patient groups? For example, some individuals may require additional behavioral treatment (or more medication) even after a prolonged period of abstinence, while others may not.

The alcoholism field needs to develop a model for combining medications and psychotherapies testable with different patient groups having varying recovery and relapse patterns. The model should provide directions related to:

(1) the compatibility of certain pharmacological agents with particular behavioral modalities, (2) the dosing schedules of drugs and behavioral treatment, and (3) the sequencing of the drugs and psychosocial treatment. In this way, findings derived from alcoholism treatment research may become more applicable to "real world" clinical settings.

To conclude, providing effective pharmacotherapy may be the impetus to integrate alcoholism treatment into the general health care system. At present, most treatment is currently provided in specialized or "carve-out" programs. This, I believe, has helped to maintain the stigma of alcoholism treatment and to reduce the accessibility of care for individuals seeking or needing help with alcohol-related problems. Incorporating alcoholism treatment into the health care system may help to destigmatize the illness, increase the accessibility of alcoholism treatment services, facilitate greater utilization of such services, and perhaps reduce disparities in insurance coverage between alcohol-related problems and other health-related disorders.

REFERENCES

Aubin, H. J. (1996). Acamprosate in clinical practice: The French experience. In M. Soyka (Ed.) *Acamprosate in relapse prevention of alcoholism*. Berlin: Springer-Verlag.

Bien, T. H., Miller, W. R., & Tonigan, J. S. (1993). Brief intervention for alcohol problems: A review. *Addiction, 88*, 315-335.

Carroll, K. M. (1997). Integrating psychotherapy and pharmacotherapy to improve drug abuse outcomes. *Addictive Behaviors, 2*, 233-246.

Cisler, R. Holder, H., Longabaugh, R., Stout, R. L, Treno, A., & Zweben, A. (1998). Actual and estimated replication costs for alcohol treatment modalities: A case study from Project MATCH. *Journal of Studies on Alcohol, 59*, 503-512.

Emrick, C. D., Tonigan, J.S., Montgomery, H., & Little, L. (1993). Alcoholics Anonymous: What is currently known? In B. D. McCrady & W. R. Miller (Eds.), *Research on alcoholics anonymous: Opportunities and alternatives* (pp. 41-78). New Brunswick, NJ Rutgers University Press.

Heather, N. (1995). Brief intervention strategies. In R. H. Hester & W. R. Miller (Eds.). *Handbook of alcoholism treatment approaches: Effective alternatives* (pp. 105-122). Needham Heights, MA: Allyn & Bacon.

Holder, H., Cisler, R., Longabaugh, R., Stout, R., Treno, A. & Zweben, A. (2000). Alcoholism treatment and medical care costs and benefits from Project MATCH, *Addiction, 95* (7). 999-1013.

Litten, R. Z., Fertig, J., & Allen, J. P. (1999). Medications development. Unpublished paper.

Longabaugh, R., & Morgenstern, J. (1999). Cognitive-behavioral coping skills therapy for alcohol dependence: Current status and future directions. *Alcohol Research & Health, 23*, 78-85.

Longabaugh, R., Wirtz, P. W., Zweben, A., & Stout, R. L. (1998). Network support for drinking, alcoholics anonymous, and long-term matching effects. *Addiction*, *93*, 1313-1333.

Miller, W. R., Meyers, R. J., & Tonigan, J. S. (1999). Engaging the unmotivated in treatment for alcohol problems: A comparison of three strategies for intervention through family members. *Journal of Consulting and Clinical Psychology*, *67*, 688-697.

Miller, W. R., Andrews, N. R., Wilbourne, P., & Bennett, M. (1998). A wealth of alternatives: Effective treatments for alcohol problems. In W. R. Miller & N. Heather (Eds.), *Treating addictive behaviors* (2nd ed., pp. 203-216). New York: Plenum Press.

O'Farrell, T. J. (1995). Marital and family therapy. In R. Hester & W. R. Miller (Eds.), *Handbook of alcoholism treatment approaches* (2nd ed., pp. 195-220). Boston: Allyn & Bacon.

O'Farrell, T. J., & Fals-Stewart, W. (1999). Treatment models and methods: Family models. In B. McCrady & E. Epstein (Eds.), *Addiction: A comprehensive guidebook for practitioners* (pp. 287-305). New York: Oxford University Press.

O'Malley, S., Jaffe, A., Chang, G., Schottenfeld, R., Meyer, R., & Rounsaville, B. (1992). Naltrexone and coping skills therapy for alcohol dependence: A controlled study. *Archives of General Psychiatry*, *49*, 881-887.

O'Malley, S., Jaffe, A., Chang, G., Rode, S., Schottenfeld, R., Meyer, R., & Rounsaville, B. (1996). Six-month follow-up of naltrexone and psychotherapy for alcohol dependence. *Archives of General Psychiatry*, *53* (3), 217-224.

Pettinati, H. M., Volpicelli, J. R., Pierce, J. D., & O'Brien, C. P. (2000). Improving naltrexone response: An intervention for medical practitioners to enhance medication compliance in alcohol dependent patients. *Journal of Addictive Diseases*, *19* (1), 71-83.

Project MATCH Research Group. (1997). Matching alcoholism treatment to client heterogeneity: Project MATCH post-treatment drinking outcomes. *Journal of Studies on Alcohol*, *58*, 7-29.

Project MATCH Research Group. (1998). Matching alcoholism treatment to client heterogeneity: Three-year drinking outcomes. *Alcoholism: Clinical & Experimental Research*, *22*, 1300-1311.

Reynolds, C. F., Frank, E., Perel, J. M., Imber, S. D., Cornes, C., Miller, M. D., Marumdar, S., Houck, P. R., Dew, M. A., Stack, J. A., Pollock, B. G., & Kupfer, D. J. (1999). Nortriptyline and interpersonal psychotherapy as maintenance therapies for recurrent major depression. *Journal of the American Medical Association*, *281* (1), 39-45.

Sass, H., Soyka, M., Mann, K., & Ziegelgansberger, W. (1996). Relapse prevention by acamprosate: Results from a placebo-controlled study on alcohol dependence. *Archives of General Psychiatry*, *53*, 673-680.

Sisson, R. W., & Azrin, N. H. (1986). Family-member involvement to initiate and promote treatment of problem drinkers. *Journal of Behavior Therapy and Experimental Psychiatry*, *17*, 15-21.

Soyka, M. (1996). Clinical efficacy of acamprosate in the treatment of alcoholism. In M. Soyka (Ed.) *Acamprosate in relapse prevention of alcoholism* (pp. 155-171). Berlin: Springer-Verlag.

Tonigan, J. S., & Toscova, R. T. (1998). Mutual help groups, Research and clinical implications. In W. R. Miller & N. Heather. *Treating addictive behaviors* (2nd ed., pp. 285-299). New York: Plenum Press.

Volpicelli, J. R., Alterman, A. I., Hayasguda, M., & O'Brien, C. P. (1992). Naltrexone in the treatment of alcohol dependence. *Archives of General Psychiatry, 49* (11), 876-880.

Volpicelli, J., Rhines, K. C., Rhines, J. S., Volpicelli, L. A., Alterman, A. I., & O'Brien, C. P. (1997). Naltrexone and alcohol dependence, Role of subject compliance. *Archives of General Psychiatry, 54*, 737-742.

Westerberg, V. S. (1998). What predicts success? In W. R. Miller & N. Heather. *Treating addictive behaviors* (2nd ed., pp. 301-315). New York: Plenum Press.

Zweben, A., Pearlman, S., & Li, S. (1983). Reducing attrition from conjoint therapy with alcoholic couples. *Drug and Alcohol Dependence, 11*, 309-319.

Zweben, A., & Barrett, D. (1993). Brief couples treatment for alcohol problems. In T. J. O'Farrell (Ed.), *Treating alcohol problems: Marital and family interventions* (pp. 353-380). New York: Guilford Press.

Neuroscience in Social Work Practice and Education

Harriette C. Johnson

SUMMARY. In the past two decades, advances in neuroscience research have revolutionized the scientific community's understanding of brain/behavior connections. Social work is now taking note of this trend. Specialists in substance abuse, addiction, and co-occurring diagnoses are beginning to relinquish long-held beliefs in mind-body dualism in favor of a truly integrated biopsychosocial understanding. This article identifies challenges related to social work and argues that neurobiological knowledge is essential for a biopsychosocial understanding of substance abuse and addiction, other mental disorders, co-occurring conditions, and human behavior. It gives examples of drawing on neurobiological knowledge for practice applications. These include educating users, families, and providers about neurobiological aspects of substance abuse (psychoeducation); using neuroscience research on mental illness and addiction to develop integrated approaches for dually diagnosed persons; and considering a range of medication options to alleviate cravings and reduce relapse. *[Article copies available for a fee from The Haworth Document Delivery Service: 1-800-342-9678. E-mail address: <getinfo@haworthpressinc.com> Website: <http://www.HaworthPress.com> © 2001 by The Haworth Press, Inc. All rights reserved.]*

Harriette C. Johnson, PhD, is Professor, University of Connecticut School of Social Work, 1798 Asylum Avenue, West Hartford, CT 06117-2698 (E-mail: hjohnson@shaysnet.com).

[Haworth co-indexing entry note]: "Neuroscience in Social Work Practice and Education." Johnson, Harriette C. Co-published simultaneously in *Journal of Social Work Practice in the Addictions* (The Haworth Social Work Practice Press, an imprint of The Haworth Press, Inc.) Vol. 1, No. 3, 2001, pp. 81-102; and: *Neurobiology of Addictions: Implications for Clinical Practice* (ed: Richard T. Spence, Diana M. DiNitto, and Shulamith Lala Ashenberg Straussner) The Haworth Social Work Practice Press, an imprint of The Haworth Press, Inc., 2001, pp. 81-102. Single or multiple copies of this article are available for a fee from The Haworth Document Delivery Service [1-800-342-9678, 9:00 a.m. - 5:00 p.m. (EST). E-mail address: getinfo@haworthpressinc.com].

KEYWORDS. Neuroscience, brain, substance abuse, addiction, dual diagnosis, co-occurring, biopsychosocial, mental, emotional

Because addiction is a brain disease, progress in fighting addiction requires knowledge of brain function. This is a significant barrier because the brain is the most complex of organs.

Adron Harris, June 12th, 2000, *Presentation: Conference on the Neurobiology of Addictions,* Austin, Texas

INTRODUCTION

Twenty years have passed since the appearance of the first book specifically for social workers on the subject of neurobiological foundations of behavior (Johnson, 1980). In the 1980s, the notion that human behavior was decisively influenced by the brain seldom penetrated the consciousness of social work educators and practitioners. When it did, it was typically dismissed as irrelevant at best, demonic at worst (Cohen, 1989).

In the past decade, particularly in the last three years, that situation has begun to change. Advances in neuroscience research in the areas of human behavior in the social environment, mental health, and substance use have revolutionized the scientific community's understanding of brain/behavior connections (US Department of Health and Human Services, 1999). Social work is now taking note of this trend. In an unprecedented front page article, the *NASW News* unequivocally endorsed a government report whose major premises include the pre-eminence of neuroscience as a basis for learning about behavior, emotions, thinking, human development, and psychiatric conditions (O'Neill, 2000; US Department of Health and Human Services, 1999). Analogous reports on substance abuse and addiction are currently in preparation by the government agencies charged with research and public information in these areas (Sirovatka, 1999, personal communication).

Yet major obstacles still exist to acceptance and incorporation of this knowledge by social work practitioners and educators (Beless, 1999; Johnson & Taylor-Brown, 1997; Saleebey 1985; 1992). Although the biopsychosocial framework for understanding psychological phenomena is widely acknowledged in social work, the tendency to focus almost exclusively on the psychological and social components is still the rule rather than the exception (Biggar & Johnson, in progress; Johnson, Atkins, Battle, Hernandez-Arata, Hesselbrock, Libassi, & Parish, 1990). Some social workers have embraced the emerging findings; others have shown reluctance to accept the new knowledge. Practitioners and educators whose thinking was molded in the era of the 1960s and 1970s, and the younger practitioners whom they have mentored, may carry with them distrust of or even antipathy to the messages of neuroscience for social work practice.

What are the challenges of neuroscience to social workers working with substance abusing and dually diagnosed clients at the inception of the 21st century? What neuroscience findings do social work practitioners need to know for direct practice? What do administrators of substance abuse programs need to know to plan and implement agency interventions? What stands in the way of our acquiring this knowledge? What strategies can we use to overcome these obstacles and bring balance to the bio-, psycho-, and social components of the biopsychosocial paradigm? This article addresses these questions. Substantive content on the brain's romances and wars with substances of abuse is presented in other articles in this volume, so is referred to only briefly here.

WHAT DO WE NEED TO LEARN FROM NEUROSCIENCE?

What knowledge do specialists in substance abuse and addictions need? What should they know to address challenges that often co-occur with abuse of alcohol and other drugs, such as mental problems, criminality, and family violence?

In order to identify specific kinds of knowledge that we need, we must first be clear about what neuroscience can and cannot offer us. Neuroscience does not have, nor have its proponents ever claimed to have, solutions to political, economic, and cultural evils such as racism, poverty, unemployment, toxic waste, workplace hazards, and inadequate public health safeguards that put millions of people at risk for substance abuse, addiction, post-traumatic stress disorder, brain damage, and exacerbations or prolongations of mental illnesses. It can only suggest remedial responses to casualties of these social ills and specify conditions necessary to prevent such casualties. In the future, neuroscience may lead to prevention.

It does have answers to some questions about the ways fetuses, infants, children, and adults develop in interaction with their environments. It can show how some specific untoward events in human brain development lead to or are associated with certain mental illnesses; how certain drugs work in specific brain structures; and what some of the biological underpinnings are for the experience of getting high. And neuroscience is beginning to show how people change from a non-addicted state to an addicted state.

Neuroscientists recognize that the knowledge they have unearthed so far is modest relative to what remains to be learned. Current knowledge is a first step toward understanding the brain, "the most complex entity in the known universe" (Hyman, 1997). Neuroscience emphasizes the influence of environmental inputs on neurological and psychological development (see for example Chugani, 1997, 1998; Meaney, Diorio et al., 1996). The question is not whether the environment has important effects on psychological function–that is a given–but rather, how such effects operate. There is simply no evidence that neuroscience is inherently narrow, reductionistic, or politically conservative. It defines its boundaries and specifies what it can and cannot offer in the way of expanding and deepening the biopsychosocial paradigm.

NEUROSCIENCE KNOWLEDGE FOR SOCIAL WORK

With respect to knowledge needed by all social workers regardless of field of practice, neuroscience can inform us about topics such as temperament (Kagan, 1994; Thomas & Chess, 1977); critical periods in development (Chugani, 1997); effects of stress on prenatal and postnatal development (Alves, Akbari, Anderson, Azmitia, McEwen, & Strand, 1997; Fuxe, Diaz, Cintra, Bhatnagaer, Tinner, Gustafsson, Ogren, & Agnati, 1996; Meaney et al., 1996); effects of maternal depression on infants (Dawson, Klinger, Panagiotides, Hill, & Spieker, 1992; Locke, Baumgart et al., 1997); resilience (Groza, 1998; Henry & Wang, 1998; Kendrick, 2000; Rutter, 1998; Werner, 1989); and affiliative behavior (including attachment, bonding, touching) (Field, Grizzle, Scafidi, & Schanberg, 1996; Field, Morrow, Valdeon, Larson, Kuhn, & Schanberg, 1992). Social workers need to know as much as they can about the ways biology-environment interactions generate emotions, behavior, and cognition. The more of this knowledge we have, the more likely we are to be aware of possible interventions that may help, and to be able to help consumers access these interventions.

Examples of questions that neuroscience researchers address are: What are the attributes of temperament (inborn, constitutional characteristics)? Are they modifiable, and if so, how? What are sensitive periods in cognitive and emotional development, and what implications does this information have for ways to respond at these critical periods to help children maximize emotional and cognitive potential? How does stress affect brain functions and brain structures from conception, through gestation, infancy, childhood, adolescence, to the end of life? How is maternal depression related to negative physiological characteristics in infants, and what preventive interventions might forestall long-term adverse effects? What are the neurobiological underpinnings of propensity for risk-taking? How is resilience manifest, and how can it be promoted? What are the biological underpinnings of mother-infant bonding, adult pair-bond formation, effects of touch, and urge to cuddle? How do these questions relate to the etiology and assessment of addiction?

Neuroscience is also critical for beginning to understand the biological underpinnings of mental disorders that co-occur with substance abuse. What are underlying differences in brain functions and structures between people who meet various criteria for "normality" (Freud, 1999; Walsh, 1993) and persons with schizophrenia, bipolar disorder, major depression, borderline or antisocial personality, phobias, or obsessive-compulsive disorder, between "normals" and people who encounter major problems in living due to impulsivity, attention-deficit, or imperviousness to social cues? Neuroscience has discovered some probable physiological and anatomical bases for these characteristics. How can pharmacological and behavioral interventions alter these conditions, and how must these interventions be modified when a psychiatric disability co-occurs with substance abuse (see for example Boulenger, Jerabek, Jolicoeur, Lavellee, Leduc, & Cadieux, 1996; Cadoret, Winokur, Langbehn, Troughton, Yates, & Stewart, 1996; Gerra, Zaimovic, Timpano, Zambelli, Begarani, Marzocchi, Ferri, Delsignore, & Brambilla, 2000; Hyman & Nestler, 1993; Leutwyler, 1996; Littrell & Schneiderhan, 1996; Matochik, Liebenauer, King, Zymanski, Cohen, & Zametkin, 1994; Weinstein, Feldtkeller, Malizia, Wilson, Bailey, & Nutt, 1998)?

HOW DOES NEUROSCIENCE ADDRESS SUBSTANCE ABUSE AND ADDICTION?

Ongoing interactions between the environment and the brain, through time, lead people to use, abuse, and become addicted to substances. Examples of questions about substance abuse and addiction that neuroscience addresses are: Why do we enjoy drugs? Why do few people relish broccoli in the way that many relish substances of abuse (Hyman, 1995)? Who is vulnerable to addiction? What are the processes by which we become addicted? Where in the addictive process might preventive interventions be most effective, and how? Why do addicted persons continue to self-destruct, despite obvious violations of self-interest such as alienating family, losing jobs, and becoming ill? What are the specific actions of drugs (both legal and illegal) in the brain? How do the chemical properties of drugs interact with the brain to warrant designation as more or less addictive? Are eating disorders addictions? How do non-ingestive or purported addictions, such as gambling or sex, develop in the brain? How can psychopharmacology help people become less drug-dependent? Is this latter question an oxymoron? These questions and many more are addressed in hundreds of research reports in the neuroscience literature (see for example Berridge, 1998; Berridge & Robinson, 1998; Koob, Sanna, & Bloom, 1998; Salamone, Cousins, & Snyder, 1997; Shippenberg & Elmer, 1998).

Neuroscience research has unearthed critical knowledge about relationships between psychological phenomena and brain functions and structures, opening "windows" to the brain for the first time in human history. The mind-body separation is an intellectual construct not borne out by scientific evidence (US Department of Health and Human Services, 1999). As it processes inputs from the environment interacting with the individual's internal environment–that is, as it processes human experience–the brain continually undergoes changes in its cellular functions and also its cellular structures. A pioneer in brain/behavior interactions, neuroscientist Eric Kandel (1979), proposed two decades ago that talk therapies, too, cause changes in the brain, specifically at synaptic connection sites.

The Fallacy of Mind-Body Dualism

Neuroscience's central premises that formerly ran counter to prevailing wisdom have now become axiomatic: (1) All psychological functions are manifestations of molecular processes, mediated by cells and larger structures in the brain and nervous system. (2) Mental illnesses are disorders of an organ, the brain, similar to diseases in other body organs such as the lungs or the kidney. (3) Inputs from the environment continually influence these molecular processes and in turn are influenced by the behavioral outputs of the organism. That is, all psychological phenomena reflect biological processes.

Psychological phenomena include not only emotions, behavior, and thinking, but also addiction: What takes place physiologically and anatomically as an individual becomes addicted; how the addicted brain differs from the person's pre-addiction brain; how these changes are manifest in affect, behavior, and cognition. Just as stresses of environmental origin can precipitate or exacerbate episodes of other illnesses (e.g., diabetic coma, heart attack), they can influence the onset or severity of substance abuse and addiction. However, short of egregious abuse or neglect, parenting styles and practices do not cause illnesses in the brain any more than they cause diabetes or heart disease, although they strongly influence children's happiness or unhappiness. In addiction, as in other mental functioning, genetically transmitted vulnerabilities interact through time with a whole range of environmental risk and protective factors, with symptoms worsening as risk factors surpass protective factors and receding as the reverse takes place.

Environmental contributors to mental disorders include not only interpersonal, cultural, economic, organizational, political, and legal factors, but biological environmental factors as well, such as lack of nutritious food, toxic pollutants, brain-affecting viruses and bacteria, and use of street and prescription drugs. In addition to triggering the onset of depression, anxiety attacks, or drug-taking behavior, the environment is critical in influencing outcomes: how severe the condition will be, how quickly it will remit, and how long the person will remain in a state of remission. This statement appears equally applicable to mental illness and addiction.

Drugs, the Brain, and Addiction

New knowledge generated by neuroscience has supported discoveries of many psychotropic medications that offer greater effectiveness and safety, combined with more benign side effect profiles, than their predecessors. Although some social workers and other specialists in addiction repudiate all kinds of medication to treat addiction, others have welcomed the helpful effects of some of these drugs for substance-abusing clients (Fayette, 2000).

Steven Hyman (1995) has offered some ways of thinking about the neurobiology of addiction that are particularly useful to social workers. They include:

1. The knowledge that drug-induced changes take place not only in physiological processes, but also in molecular structures in the brain. Ongoing drug use causes brain changes that commandeer motivational systems. Chronic use of drugs causes long-lived molecular changes in the signaling properties of neurons, for example, by decreasing the number of dopamine receptors on the post-synaptic neuron. Depending on the drug and the circuits involved, these adaptations have different effects on behavior and different time-courses of initiation and decay. This biological process of usurpation is extraordinarily powerful and offers a helpful explanation of why staying clean and sober is so difficult.

2. The concept of vulnerability. Vulnerability is a more complicated concept than we sometimes think, because the same individual has fluctuating levels of vulnerability in different environments and life situations at different times in his or her life. Environmental and biological risk factors emerge and recede, appear and subside, all through life.

3. Long-term changes resulting from chronic drug use (sometimes even short-term use) in brain centers that control three functions: somatic

functions, rewards and pleasures, and emotional memories. Only a few drugs involve what Hyman calls somatic dependence, but almost all drugs of abuse are believed to induce the other two kinds of long-term changes in the brain.

Somatic dependence is defined by the presence of changes that appear in withdrawal as unequivocally physical symptoms, particularly for three types of drugs: alcohol (e.g., tremor, hypertension, grand mal seizure, tachycardia, delusions, hallucinations), opiates (e.g., severe muscle cramps, bone ache, tearing, diarrhea, hypothermia or hyperthermia, insomnia, nausea, goose-flesh), and caffeine (headache, fatigue, nausea). These somatic manifestations may last for days, weeks, or longer, but ordinarily are time-limited.

Changes in brain reward and pleasure pathways, in microanatomic structures as well as physiological processes, involve motivation and volition. Motivational aspects of withdrawal are dysphoria (feeling blue, sad, depressed), anhedonia (inability to experience pleasure in pursuits enjoyed prior to becoming addicted), and cravings. The person suffering from these feelings experiences a change in behavioral priorities. Now, getting the drug of abuse becomes the most important goal in life.

With sufficient dose, frequency, and chronicity, a vulnerable person becomes addicted (i.e., his or her brain is changed). For example, in cocaine addiction, the user is flooded by his or her own dopamine in response to using. Over time, the sledgehammering of the brain's dopamine system by the drug triggers an effort to restore homeostasis. Genetic materials (DNA, RNA) are "transcribed" and "translated" (read out to make a copy and then converted into protein), as the brain attempts to adapt to too much dopamine. The adaptive mechanism involves reducing the number of dopamine receptors in some of the dopamine pathways. Now users no longer have enough receptors for dopamine to experience some of the everyday pleasures they enjoyed prior to addiction. The psychic pain that addicts experience when withdrawing is just as real and just as physical as the pain of somatic withdrawal, but its forms of expression are largely evident in psychological functions (emotional, cognitive, behavioral). In an addicted state, individuals may strive to avoid dysphoria (emotional pain) by denial or rationalization (*cognitions* that support avoidance of or escape from abstinence-generated emotional pain), and compulsive drug-seeking (*behavior* that supports avoidance of or escape from abstinence-generated emotional pain). Thus the distinction between physical and psychological addiction is a myth. All addiction has physical underpinnings, and all psychological phenomena have physical underpinnings. This may be the most difficult concept for social workers to accept, creating as it does cognitive dissonance with the dualistic developmental theories that still are a core aspect of social work professional education.

These changes in brain reward systems can last for months and years. The third kind of change, the laying down of emotional memories, is perhaps the most refractory kind of change in neuronal structure and function, because emotional memories ordinarily last a lifetime. Over the life course many memories are eventually lost through decay of memory traces in the brain. However, memories of powerful experiences remain. Cues evoke memories of intensely pleasurable experiences (leading, in the case of drugs, to cravings and relapse) or intensely painful experiences (leading to traumatic flooding as in post-traumatic stress disorder). These memories are referred to as "privileged" memories because they pre-empt other less potent memories to take precedence in the individual's emotional state and in motivating behavior.

Several brain circuits and structures are believed to be involved in these latter two types of long-term changes (reward, pleasure, and motivation; emotional memories), with different drugs being processed by different configurations of brain systems. Prominent among these are the mesolimbic dopamine pathway (ventral tegmental area, nucleus accumbens), the basal ganglia (caudate nucleus, putamen, globus pallidus, substantia nigra), thalamic nuclei, and prefrontal cortex.

Drugs of abuse mimic natural transmitters whose chemical structures resemble theirs, and sometimes fool receptors programmed for a specific natural transmitter into accepting them instead. Each drug works through a specific chain of molecular events to impart its effects on the individual. Each drug has its own special neurotransmitters or neuromodulators through which it operates in chain reactions (see for example Johnson, 1999, p. 40). Dopamine is frequently involved in these chain reactions, as well as neuropeptides, GABA (gamma-aminobutyric acid), acetylcholine, serotonin, adenosine, and other transmitters and neuromodulators.

Addiction and Individual Responsibility

The perennial question about addicts' responsibility for their behavior is important here. The brain of an addict is compromised. Yet acknowledging that addicts are not to blame for the fact that they have become addicted in the first place (because their own particular configuration of vulnerabilities led them to this compromised state) does not imply that they have no responsibility for continuing drug-taking behavior. No matter what the reasons for acquiring an addictive illness, only they can take effective action to overcome its adverse effects by initiating a recovery process. Similar reasoning applies to other diseases. Although people usually are not blamed for having heart disease that was an outgrowth of fatty diet and sedentary lifestyle, only they can modify their behavior to alter the future course of the disease.

Just as family members, doctors, and friends can support health-promoting be-havior with respect to the heart, family members of addicts, peers, and service pro-viders can supply supports for sobriety, but only the individual is responsible for continuing or ceasing drug use. Psychosocial interventions such as Alcoholics Anonymous, Narcotics Anonymous, other peer support groups, motivational in-terviewing, relapse prevention coaching, and cognitive-behavioral therapy, act neurobiologically by propping up intact parts of the brain that can overcome com-pelling urges to use drugs that emanate from the compromised part of the brain.

WHY DO SOCIAL WORKERS NEED THIS INFORMATION?

One reason is that psychoeducation, commonly utilized in addiction treatment settings, requires knowledge about neurobiological underpinnings of substance abuse and other mental disorders (Foote, Seligman, Magura, Handelsman, Rosenblum, Lovejoy, Arrington, & Stimmel, 1994; Rosen-Chase & Dyson, 1999). Although empirical studies are lacking that could show which aspects of psychoeducation account for its favorable performance on outcome measures, it appears to play a major role in answering plaguing questions for sufferers ("What's wrong with me? Why am I the way I am?") as well as their family's que-ries ("What's wrong with our loved one? What did I do to cause this?").

Another reason is that failure to learn new knowledge constitutes violation of the NASW code of ethics, which requires social workers to "keep current with emerging knowledge . . . and fully use . . . research evidence in their practice" (National Association of Social Workers, 1996). The incorporation of neurosci-ence's answers to these questions may significantly expand the range of choices of interventions considered by providers and clients alike, so that the worker's failure to become conversant with this knowledge deprives clients of potential help. For example, learning how a medication may diminish cravings, as well as understanding the process by which cravings developed in the first place, may lead an addict to accept a trial of medication to see if it helps. Without this infor-mation, workers or clients may reject such an option out of hand, based on the reasonable supposition that treating an addiction with yet another chemical can only compound dependence on drugs. Unless we know something about neurobiological underpinnings of eating disorders or heroin use, how can we un-derstand medical rationales for proposed interventions? How can we know when to challenge such proposals? How can we explain the recommendations of a treatment team to an addicted person that he or she take a selective serotonin reuptake inhibitor (SSRI) or naltrexone for relief from depression and cravings?

With respect to professional self-interest, social workers need to become "neurobiology-literate," like providers from other disciplines such as medicine, psychiatry, nursing, and psychology that routinely include basics of neurobiology in their training. Isn't it time for social workers to reject the role of handmaiden in the human services and step up to the plate as equal players? Shouldn't we have the scientific knowledge that other disciplines doing work similar to ours have, knowledge necessary to suggest, initiate, and evaluate the effects of biological interventions, or, conversely, the effects of the absence of biological interventions? Shouldn't we be equipped to take an active role in debating current neuroscience controversies relevant to our fields of practice, such as the roles of different brain systems in developing addictions to cocaine, alcohol, food, or gambling (see Jill Littrell's article in this volume, and Berridge & Robinson, 1998; Salamone, Cousins, & Snyder, 1997)?

A final reason for acquiring this knowledge is perhaps more philosophical than pragmatic. Shouldn't we be educated, up-to-date consumers of the stream of research knowledge about human psychological functioning that continues to emerge at an increasing rate? Shouldn't we join the neuroscientists and follow, step by step, the controversies their studies engender, such as the role of dopamine in the range of addictions that we encounter (see for example Littrell, this volume; Salamone, Cousins, & Snyder, 1997)?

WHAT OBSTACLES STAND IN THE WAY OF SOCIAL WORKERS LEARNING THIS INFORMATION?

Forces contributing to antipathy to a biological understanding of psychological functioning are suggested by Saleebey (1985), such as suspicion that the biological knowledge base conceals a conservative political agenda, the profession's long history of preference for focus on interpersonal relationships, prevalence of theoretical models conceived before knowledge about biological foundations of behavior were well articulated, perceived lack of expertise, and turf issues.

Reluctance to Integrate New Knowledge

The history of beliefs about mental disorders may help explain the resistance among many social work educators to the new knowledge. Prior to the arrival of Freud's theories in the U.S. in the 1920s, physicians believed that schizophrenia and other mental disorders were biological diseases of the body organ called the brain. Freud, himself a neurologist, believed this as well early in his career, but the crudeness of scientific tools available in that era frustrated him and led him to develop theories unconnected to the brain (his constructs of "physical" entities such as id, ego, and superego were metaphorical only).

From the 1920s to the 1960s, a dichotomous theory of the etiology of mental disorders (and by extension, addictive disorders) captured professional imagination, and the American consciousness with it. One set of disorders of the mind was called "organic" (e.g., senile dementia, drug intoxication, and mental retardation). All others were subsumed under the rubric "functional." Although the field of addiction appears to have given up explicit Freudian constructs as etiological explanations, the persistence of a dualist view of psychological phenomena suggests that its influence still operates. For example, the most widely used social work textbook for required courses in human behavior and the social environment (HBSE), according to a recent survey (Biggar & Johnson, in progress), states that drug dependence "may be physical, psychological, or both" (Zastrow & Kirst-Ashman, 1999, p. 451). That is, the authors appear to believe that physical and psychological addictions are separate and different, and that psychological addiction can exist independent of the physical body. By contrast, contemporary neuroscience has validated that psychological phenomena associated with becoming addicted, such as reordering motivational priorities and laying down emotional memories, are all based in physiological actions in the brain.

In the mid-20th century, Skinner's operant conditioning appealed to many in psychology, whose tradition of scientific inquiry made it receptive to experimentally validated knowledge. Social work, however, was suspicious of and hostile to anything that appeared to reduce behavior to a stimulus-response model. Despite a few early social work proponents of behavioral approaches (Schwartz, 1983; Rose, 1977; Thomas, 1967), its influence was minimal until the last decade of the 20th century.

Family systems theories also ascended to pre-eminence in the 1970s and 1980s, promoting the concept that individual "disorders" seldom are real entities. Rather, they are individual symptoms of underlying family dysfunction for which the individual with the supposed disorder functions as the symptom carrier. The dualistic premise was paramount in family systems theory, as it located the origin of all psychological problems in family interaction. However, the merit of concepts such as "enmeshment," "triangulation," and "codependence," although popular among therapists, have been questioned. Not only do they usually reflect an exclusively interpersonal framework of etiology that leaves out biological factors, but they also have unfairly blamed partners or parents for substance abuse and addiction (Johnson, Cournoyer, Fisher, Flynn, Moriarty, Richert, Stanek, Stockford, & Yirigian, 2000).

Cognitive psychology, emphasizing the influence of thinking on emotional states, became well-known in the 1970s under the leadership of therapists such as Aaron Beck (Wright & Beck, 1983) and Albert Ellis (Ellis, McInerrey, DiGuiseppi, & Yeager, 1988). Recognizing their respective limitations during the 1970s and 1980s, cognitive and behavioral approaches merged in the 1970s and early 1980s into "cognitive-behavioral" practice (Caroll, 1998; Meichenbaum, 1993). This approach has been widely utilized by psychologists in the field of addictions research and treatment and, finally in the mid-1990s, espoused growing numbers of social work practitioners and educators, particularly in the addictions field. Cognitive-behavioral psychology, unlike psychoanalytic and family systems theories, is consistent with and is increasingly being integrated with neuroscience (den Boer, 2000; Gorman, Kent, Sullivan, & Coplan, 2000; Hollander, Buchalter, & DeCaria, 2000).

Social work became excited about general systems theory in the late 1960s and early 1970s, as a conceptual framework for understanding human behavior that could weave together macro dimensions, so emphasized in the 1960s, with micro dimensions of psychological functioning (Miller, 1978). However, general systems theory fell into disrepute. Though it offered a comprehensive biopsychosocial perspective, it lacked specific tools for translating that perspective into real work with real people.

During these years, social work's attachment to psychological dualism was accompanied by rising antipathy to the medical metaphor, a reaction to the widespread acceptance of the "diagnostic" approach of ego psychology and other psychoanalytic derivatives (Miller, 1980; Pilsecker, 1983; Weick, 1983). A central tenet of these approaches was the belief that most troubled states arise from pathogenic forces in the individual's early environment–forces equated with deficient or toxic parenting, usually by the mother (Caplan & Hall-McCorquodale, 1985). Practitioners using this theoretical frame cast themselves in the role of "head doctors" who diagnosed and treated psychological and addictive disorders assumed to be non-biological in nature. Thus the medical model was truly a metaphor, since it was applied to problems assumed to be unambiguously non-medical. This medical metaphor applied to non-biological phenomena acquired a bad name, as did biology itself. Feminists and human rights activists called on the social work profession to repudiate the medical model and the notion that inborn biological factors could cause or contribute to behavioral or emotional problems (Johnson et al., 1990).

Distaste for the Medical Model

Several questions are still at issue. What is the role of the "medical model" in contemporary practice? Are addictive states really diseases? Are mental disorders really diseases? Are conditions that meet criteria for *DSM-IV* diagnoses (American Psychiatric Association, 1994) really even "disorders" (Wakefield, 1999)? Judgments about intensity and duration of signs and symptoms necessary to qualify for diagnoses such as substance abuse disorder, major depression, and attention-deficit/hyperactivity disorder are arbitrary, not scientific. Thresholds for mental "disorders" have been set by professional convention. Yet the same is true for other areas of medicine (US Department of Health and Human Services, 1999, p. 39). For example, ten years ago a serum cholesterol of 200 was considered normal, whereas today the same number alarms medical practitioners.

Despite the thorny scientific and philosophical issues inherent in a disease model for constellations of psychological characteristics, knowledge about mechanisms by which these conditions occur is usually important in developing effective interventions. Learning about mechanisms underlying substance abuse, addiction, and mental disturbance requires knowledge about the fundamentals of neuroscience (Harris, 2000). Unfortunately, offensiveness of the medical model to many practitioners often results in dismissal of science and repudiation of interventions that have been demonstrated to offer the most effective help for a given condition (Breggin & Breggin, 1994; Eberle, 1996). Issues surrounding the medical model are related to the theoretical frameworks social workers and other professionals draw on in their choice of interventions (Johnson et al., 2000; Johnson & Renaud, 1997). Thus the historical antecedents that deter receptiveness to state-of-the-art knowledge must be made explicit, so that we can identify the real ethical and intellectual dilemmas we face today.

What Strategies Can We Develop to Overcome These Obstacles?

Strategies must be geared to the interrelated goals of finding a compatible conceptual framework that links neuroscience to social work, expanding our own knowledge, educating other social work educators and practitioners, educating students, and working politically to expand requirements by CSWE and by state licensing boards for content on neurobiological aspects of psychological functioning.

A first step in overcoming the obstacles considered above is to find or create a conceptual framework that can integrate neuroscience findings with the multiple other sources of knowledge drawn on by social workers. Human behavior and social work practice theories have long enjoyed a privileged position in the hierarchy of social work educational priorities. Yet the Surgeon General's Report (US Department of Health and Human Services, 1999) asserts that all existing *theories* of human behavior and human psychological development have failed to explain how children grow into mentally healthy adults (or, by extension, mentally disordered adults). The findings of the meta-analysis of existing prospective longitudinal research on human development by Kagan and

Zentner (1996) support this conclusion. The Report calls for development of a new theory that is consistent with current scientific knowledge, notably *empirical advances in neuroscience* and *behavioral research* (US Department of Health and Human Services, 1999, p. 129). The behavioral research to which it refers is not limited to individuals or even families. It also comprises macrosystem factors (economic, political) and mesosystems (organizations, social groups) (Bronfenbrenner, 1979), variables often studied by disciplines such as epidemiology, sociology, economics, political science, social work, and social psychology. Examples of addiction-related research that address some of these variables are found in the work of Henggeler and colleagues (Henggeler, Pickrel, Brondino, & Crouch, 1996; Henggeler, Schoenwald, Borduin, Rowland, & Cunningham, 1998; Huey, Henggeler, Brondino, & Pickrel, 1996; Randall, Henggeler, Pickrel, & Brondino, 2000).

A second step toward overcoming obstacles involves educating ourselves about neuroscience research findings pertinent to human development at all ages, mental health and mental disorders, and substance abuse and addiction, and about fundamentals of brain systems (structures and functions of different brain regions and pathways), structures and functions of neurons, and effects of different classes of legal and illegal drugs on the brain.

A third step is to make this information available to practitioners, social work educators and students, packaged so our colleagues can become neurobiology-literate without excessive expenditure of time and energy. In addition to social work faculty, doctoral students are critical targets for this effort, as they can be expected to assume teaching responsibilities in social work education. Venues can include faculty development workshops at universities and annual program meetings of the Council on Social Work Education, doctoral colloquia, interdisciplinary conferences on neuroscience for human services, and dissemination of curriculum materials that are easy for faculty to understand and use, with grants to support these initiatives. Marketing such efforts would be greatly enhanced by sponsorship or at least endorsement by CSWE and NASW. At the local level, continuing education workshops can be offered to community practitioners.

THE EPIDEMIOLOGICAL MODEL

In our view, the "new" theory called for by the Surgeon General's Report (US Department of Health and Human Services, 1999) already exists, although it could benefit from expansion and elaboration. The conceptual model developed in the field of epidemiology–based on the understanding that all mental difficulties arise from ongoing interactions through time of biological and environmental risk and protective factors–has advanced the biopsychosocial or person-in-environment approach so long advocated by social work. The epidemiological model plugs in empirical data to identify risk and protective factors, specifies a range of possible biological and environmental risk and protective factors, and captures the notion of change through time by emphasizing that the configuration of risk and protective factors is continuously subject to alteration by the introduction, removal, or modification of a risk or protective factor. In substance abuse and addiction, the point at which the delicate balance between risk and protective factors is upset by adding or strengthening a risk factor, or losing or weakening a protective factor, is the moment in time at which a person becomes a "substance abuser" (however defined), as contrasted with "substance user." The sequelae of substance abuse, i.e., dependence or addiction, are natural consequences of the influences of ongoing risk factors (both biological and environmental), inadequately countered by protective factors.

The roles of the social worker, expressed in epidemiological terms, are to help diminish risk factors or lessen their effects, while developing protective factors or enhancing their effects. Is it possible that the epidemiological model, as simple as it appears, could be the core of the elusive theory that the authors of the Surgeon General's Report have yet to identify? It is science-based; no other theory except behavioral can claim a substantial empirical base. It takes cognizance of developmental factors, since new demands, maturing capabilities, new roles with their related new responsibilities, or other challenges over the lifespan, may be either risk factors or protective factors, and may be activated at any point in the lifespan.

As a core practice theory, the epidemiological model converges with social work's so-called strengths and empowerment perspectives. It calls for social workers and other mental health practitioners to help clients identify and maximize protective factors. In the roles of therapist, case manager, or administrator, the same principles apply. The posture of collaboration and consultation, rather than a professional expert ministering to (weaker, less powerful, lower status) service users, fits very well with a risk factor/protective factor understanding of etiology. In substance abuse and dependence, as in other mental and behavioral disorders, social workers offer their expertise for clients to consider, clients offer their own expertise for social workers to consider, and together they develop understanding of the client's problems, strengths, and needs, and the environment's capacities to meet those needs. They brainstorm together about how to make best use of the client's own capabilities and to exploit the capacities of the environment. No one is expected to have answers. The participants work together to formulate questions and to experiment with possible solutions.

The epidemiological model is also egalitarian and universalistic. It assumes that all human beings have strengths and weaknesses and that good fortune is not equitably distributed. Everyone is subjected to risk factors and (almost) everyone is blessed with protective factors. The theory does not categorize individuals with a high preponderance of risk factors as having "severe pathology," but rather looks at biology/environment interactions through time, recognizing that the people's illnesses, be they addictive, mental, or co-occurring, are realistically attributable to a bad roll of the dice. The epidemiological model as a unifying mental health practice theory is also congruent with our knowledge base at the beginning of the 21st century.

CONCLUSION

Neurobiology is beginning to be integrated into social work education. However, the changes advocated by the author cannot be expected to occur easily or quickly, owing to both the ideological and institutional obstacles discussed above. Political strategies for expanding importation of neuroscience content into social work curricula are clearly called for, as social work still lags behind psychology and nursing with respect to this goal. Were CSWE to require meaningful inclusion of neurobiological content in HBSE courses, the profession would probably stop dragging its feet and remedy its deficiencies in short order. A similar effect would take place if licensure (state and national) required such content. Substance abusers, dually diagnosed persons, and their families would be the winners of such policy advances, that would accelerate the profession's acceptance of the need for change and incorporation of neurobiological knowledge into social work practice in behalf of this large population.

REFERENCES

Albee, G. W. (1982). The politics of nature and nurture. *American Journal of Community Psychology, 10* (1), 4-30.

Alves, S. E., Akbari, H. M., Anderson, G. M., Azmitia, E. C., McEwen, B. C., & Strand, F. L. (1997). Neonatal ACTH administration elicits long-term changes in forebrain monoamine innervation. Subsequent disruptions in hypothalamic-pituitary-adrenal and gonadal function. *Annals of the New York Academy of Sciences, 814,* 226-251.

American Psychiatric Association. (1994). *Diagnostic and Statistical Manual of Mental Disorders, 4th ed.* Washington, DC: American Psychiatric Press.

Beless, D. W. (1999). Foreword. *Psyche, Synapse and Substance: The Role of Neurobiology in Emotions, Behavior, Thinking, and Addiction for Non-Scientists.* Greenfield, MA: Deerfield Valley Publishing, p. ii.

Berridge, K. C. (1995). Food reward: Brain substrates of wanting and liking. *Neuroscience and Biobehavioral Reviews*, 20(1), 1-25.

Berridge, K. C., & Robinson, T. E. (1998). What is the role of dopamine in reward: Hedonic impact, reward learning, or incentive salience? *Brain Research Reviews*, *28*, 309-369.

Biggar, M., & Johnson, H. C. (in progress). Have social work faculty embraced neuroscience?

Boulenger, J. P., Jerabek, I., Jolicoeur, F. B., Lavellee, Y. J., Leduc, R., & Cadieux, A. (1996). Elevated plasma levels of neuropeptide Y in patients with panic disorder. *American Journal of Psychiatry*, *153*(1), 114-116.

Breggin, P., & Breggin, G. R. (1994). *The War Against Children: How the Drugs, Programs, and Theories of the Psychiatric Establishment Are Threatening America's Children with a Medical "Cure" for Violence*. New York: St. Martin's Press.

Bronfenbrenner, U. (1979). *The Ecology of Human Development: Experiments by Nature and Design*. Cambridge, MA: Harvard University Press.

Bruns, E. J., & Burchard, D. (2000). Impact of respite care services for families with children experiencing emotional and behavioral problems. *Children's Services: Social Policy, Research, and Practice, 3*(1), 39-61.

Burchard, J. D, Atkins, M., & Burchard, S. N. (1996). Wraparound services. In Jacobson, J. W. & Mulick, J. A., (Eds.). *Manual of Diagnosis and Professional Practice in Mental Retardation,* pp. 403-411. Washington DC: American Psychological Association.

Cadoret, R. J., Winokur, G., Langbehn, D., Troughton, E., Yates, W. R., & Stewart, M. A. (1996). Depression spectrum disease, I: The role of gene-environment interaction. *American Journal of Psychiatry*, *153*(7), 892-899.

Caplan, P. J., & Hall-McCorquodale, I. (1985). Mother-blaming in major clinical journals. *American Journal of Orthopsychiatry*, *55*, 345-353.

Caroll, K. M. (1998). A cognitive-behavioral approach: Treating cocaine addiction. US Department of Health and Human Services, National Institutes of Health, National Institutes of Drug Abuse 98-4308.

Chugani, H. T. (1997). Neuroimaging of developmental nonlinearity and developmental pathologies, pp. 187-195, *Developmental Neuroimaging: Mapping the Development of Brain and Behavior*, In R. W. Thatcher, G. R. Lyon, J. Rumsey & N. Krasnegor (Eds.), San Diego: Academic Press.

Chugani, H. T. (1998). Unpublished data. Reported by M. Talbot, Attachment theory: The ultimate experiment. *New York Times Magazine* (May 24), 24-54.

Cohen, D. (1989). The biological basis of schizophrenia: The evidence reconsidered. *Social Work*, *34*(3), 255-257.

Council on Social Work Education. (1992). *Curriculum Policy Statement*. Draft revisions 2000. Washington, DC: CSWE.

Dawson, G., Klinger, L. G., Panagiotides, H., Hill, D., & Spieker, S. (1992). Frontal lobe activity and affective behavior of infants of mothers with depressive symptoms. *Child Development*, *63*(3), 725-737.

Den Boer, J. A. (2000). Social anxiety disorder/social phobia: Epidemiology, diagnosis, neurobiology, and treatment. *Comprehensive Psychiatry*, *41*(6), 405-415.

Eberle, A. (1996). Perspectives: War on children revisited. *Claiming Children* (letter), newsletter of the Federation of Families for Children's Mental Health.

Ellis, A., McInerrey, J. F., DiGuiseppi, R., & Yeager, R. J. (1998). Albert Ellis on rational emotive behavior therapy. *American Journal of Psychotherapy, 51*(3), 309-316.

Fayette, S. (2000). Personal communication. Northampton, MA.

Field, T., Grizzle, N., Scafidi, F., & Schanberg, S. (1996). Massage and relaxation therapies: Effects on depressed adolescent mothers. *Adolescence, 31*(124), 903-911.

Field, T., Morrow, C., Valdeon, C., Larson, S., Kuhn, C., & Schanberg, S. (1992). Massage reduces anxiety in child and adolescent psychiatric patients. *Journal of the American Academy of Child and Adolescent Psychiatry, 31*(1), 125-131.

Foote, J., Seligman, M., Magura, S., Handelsman, L., Rosenblum, A., Lovejoy, M., Arrington, K., & Stimmel, B. (1994). An enhanced positive reinforcement model for the severely impaired cocaine abuser. *Journal of Substance Abuse Treatment, 11*(6), 525-539.

Freud, S. (1999). The social construction of normality. *Families in Society*, July/August, 333-339.

Fuxe, K., Diaz, R., Cintra, A., Bhatnagar, M., Tinner, B., Gustafsson, J. A., Ogren, S., & Agnati, L. F. (1996). On the role of glucocorticoid receptors in brain plasticity. *Cellular and Molecular Neurobiology, 16*(2), 239-258.

Gerra, G., Zaimovic, A., Timpano, M., Zambelli, U., Begarani, M., Marzocchi, G. F., Ferri, M., Delsignore, R., & Brambilla, F. (2000). Neuroendocrine correlates of temperament traits in abstinent opiate addicts. *Journal of Substance Abuse, 11*(4), 337-54.

Gorman, J. M., Kent, J. M., Sullivan, G. M., & Coplan, J. D. (2000). Neuroanatomical hypothesis of panic disorder, revised. *American Journal of Psychiatry, 157*(4), 493-505.

Gould, K. H. (1987). Life model versus conflict model: A feminist perspective. *Social Work, 32*(4): 346-351.

Groza, V. (1998). Cited in Talbot, M., Attachment: The ultimate experiment. *New York Times Magazine*, (May 24), 24-54.

Harris, A. (2000). Presentation: Conference on the Neurobiology of Addiction, June 12th. Austin, Texas.

Henggeler, S. W., Pickrel, S. G., Brondino, M. J., & Crouch, J. L. (1996). Eliminating (almost) treatment dropout of substance abusing or dependent delinquents through home-based multisystemic therapy. *American Journal of Psychiatry, 153*(3), 427-8.

Henggeler, S. W., Schoenwald, S. K., Borduin, C. M., Rowland, M. D., & Cunningham, P. B. (1998). *Multisystemic Treatment of Antisocial Behavior in Children and Adolescents*. New York: Guilford.

Henry, J. P., & Wang, S. (1998). Effects of early stress on adult affiliative behavior. *Psychoneuroendocrinology, 23*(8), 863-873.

Hollander, E., Buchalter, A. J., & DeCaria, C. M. (2000). Pathological gambling. *Psychiatric Clinics of North America, 23*(3), 629-642.

Huey, S. J., Jr., Henggeler, S. W., Brondino, M. J., & Pickrel, S. G. (1996). Mechanisms of change in multisystemic therapy: Reducing delinquent behavior through therapist adherence and improved family and peer functioning. *Journal of Consulting & Clinical Psychology, 68*(3), 451-467.

Hyman, S. E. (1995). What is addiction? *Harvard Medical Alumni Review*, Winter.

Hyman, S. E. (1997). *Science and Treatment.* Video on Neuroscience and Mental Health, National Alliance for the Mentally Ill.

Hyman, S. E., & Nestler, E. J. (1993). *Molecular Foundations of Psychiatry.* Washington, DC: American Psychiatric Press.

Johnson, A. M., & Taylor-Brown, S. (1997). *Social Work Education Reporter.* Alexandria, VA: Council on Social Work Education.

Johnson, H. C. (1980). *Human Behavior in the Social Environment: New Perspectives. Vol I. Behavior, Psychopathology, and the Brain.* New York: Curriculum Concepts.

Johnson, H. C. (1999). *Psyche, Synapse, and Substance: The Role of Neurobiology in Emotions, Behavior, Thinking, and Addiction for Non-Scientists.* Greenfield, MA: Deerfield Valley Publishing.

Johnson, H. C., Atkins, S. P., Battle, S. F., Hernandez-Arata, L., Hesselbrock, M., Libassi, M. F., & Parish, M. S. (1990). Strengthening the "bio" in the biopsychosocial paradigm. *Journal of Social Work Education, 26*(2), 109-123.

Johnson, H. C., Cournoyer, D. E., Fisher, G. A., McQuillan, B. E., Moriarty, S., Richert, A. L., Stanek, E. J., Stockford, C. L., & Yirigian, B. R. (2000). Children's emotional and behavioral disorders: Attributions of parental responsibility by professionals. *American Journal of Orthopsychiatry, 70*(3), 327-339.

Johnson, H. C., & Renaud, E. F. (1997). Professional beliefs about parents of children with mental and emotional disabilities: A cross-discipline comparison. *Journal of Emotional and Behavioral Disorders, 5*(3), 149-161.

Kagan, J. (1994). *The Nature of the Child, 10th Anniversary Edition.* New York: Basic Books.

Kagan, J. & Zentner, M. (1996). Early childhood predictors of adult psychopathology. *Harvard Review of Psychiatry,* pp. 341-350.

Kaminer, W. (1995). Chances are you're codependent too. In M. Babcock and M.C. McKay (Eds.), *Challenging Codependency: Feminist Critiques.* Toronto: University of Toronto Press.

Kandel, E. (1979). Psychotherapy and the single synapse. The impact of psychiatric thought on neurobiologic research. *New England Journal of Medicine*, Nov. 8, *301*(19), 1028-1037.

Kendrick, K. M. (2000). Oxytocin, motherhood, and bonding. *Experimental Physiology*, 85 Spec No., 111S-124S.

Koob, G. F., Sanna, P. P., & Bloom, F. E. (1998). Neuroscience of addiction. *Neuron, 21*, 467-476.

Leutwyler, K. (1996). Paying attention: The controversy over ADHD and the drug Ritalin is obscuring a real look at the disorder and its underpinnings. *Scientific American, 275*(2), 12;14.

Littrell, R. A., & Schneiderhan, M. (1996). The neurobiology of schizophrenia. *Pharmacotherapy, 16*(6 PT 2), 143S-147S; discussion 166S-168S.

Locke, R., Baumgart, S., Locke, K., Goodstein, M., Thies, C., & Greenspan, J. (1997). Effect of maternal depression on premature infant health during initial hospitalization. *Journal of the American Osteopathic Association, 97*(3), 145-149.

Matochik, J. A., Liebenauer, L. L., King, A. C., Zymanski, H. V., Cohen, R. M., & Zametkin, A. J. (1994). Cerebral glucose metabolism in adults with attention deficit hyperactivity disorders after chronic stimulant treatment. *American Journal of Psychiatry, 151*(5), 658-664.

Meaney, M. J., Diorio, J., Frances, D., Widdowson, J., LaPlante, P., Cladji, C., Sharma, S., Seckl, J. R., & Plotsky, P. M. (1996). Early environmental regulation of forebrain glucocorticoid receptor gene expression: Implications for adrenocortical responses to stress. *Developmental Neuroscience, 18*(1-2), 49-72.

Meichenbaum, D. H. (1993). Changing conceptions of cognitive behavior modification: Retrospect and prospect. *Journal of Consulting and Clinical Psychology 61*(2), 202-204.

Miller, J. G. (1978). *Living Systems.* New York: McGraw Hill.

Miller, W. L. (1980). Casework and the medical metaphor. *Social Work, 25*(4), 281-285.

National Association of Social Workers Delegate Assembly. (1996). Code of ethics of the National Association of Social Workers. Washington, DC: Author.

National Association of Social Workers. (1997). *Code of Ethics.* Washington DC: NASW.

O'Neill, J. V. (2000). Surgeon General's report lauded. *NAWS News, 45*(2), 1, 6.

Pilsecker, C. (1983). The mischievous medical model. *Social Work 1,* 70-85.

Randall, J., Henggeler, S. W., Pickrel, S. G., & Brondino, M. J. (2000). Psychiatric comorbidity and the 16-month trajectory of substance-abusing and substance-dependent juvenile offenders. *Journal of Consulting and Clinical Psychology, 68*(3), 451-467.

Rose, S. D. (1977). *Group Theory: A Behavioral Approach.* Englewood Cliffs, NJ: Prentice-Hall.

Rosenblatt, A., & Waldfogel, D. (Eds.) (1983). *Handbook of Clinical Social Work.* San Francisco: Jossey-Bass.

Rosen-Chase, C., & Dyson, V. (1999). Treatment of nicotine dependence in the chronic mentally ill. *Journal of Substance Abuse Treatment, 16*(4), 315-320.

Rutter, M. (1998). Developmental catch-up and deficit following adoption after severe early global privation. *Journal of Child Psychology and Psychiatry, 39*(4), 465-476.

Salamone, J. D., Cousins, M. S., & Snyder, B. J. (1997). Behavioral functions of nucleus accumbens dopamine: Empirical and conceptual problems with the anhedonia hypothesis. *Neuroscience Biobehavioral Review, 21*(3), 341-359.

Saleebey, D. (1985). In clinical social work practice, is the body politic? *Social Service Review, 59*(4), 578-592.

Saleebey, D. (1992). Biology's challenge to social work: Embodying the person-in-environment perspective. *Social Work, 37*(2), 112-118.

Schwartz, A. (1983). Behavioral principles and approaches. In *Handbook of Clinical Social Work,* pp. 202-228, A. Rosenblatt and D. Waldfogel (Eds.), San Francisco: Jossey-Bass.

Shippenberg, T. S., & Elmer, G. I. (1998). The neurobiology of opiate reinforcement. *Critical Reviews in Neurobiology, 12*(4), 267-303.

Sirovatka, P. (1999). Personal communication. Science Editor, Office of Science Policy and Program Planning, National Institute of Mental Health.

Talbot, M. (1998). Attachment: The ultimate experiment. *New York Times Magazine*, (May 24), 24-54.

Thomas, A., & Chess, S. (1977). *Temperament and Development.* New York: Brunner/Mazel.

Thomas, E. J. (Ed.). (1967). *Sociobehavioral Approach and Applications to Social Work.* New York: Council on Social Work Education.

US Department of Health and Human Services. (1999). *Mental Health: A Report of the Surgeon General.* Rockville, MD: US Dept of HHS, Substance Abuse and Mental Health Services Administration, Center for Mental Health Services, National Institutes of Health, National Institute of Mental Health.

Wakefield, J. C. (1999). The concept of disorder as a foundation for the DSM's theory-neutral nosology: Response to Follette and Houts, Part 2. *Behavior Research and Therapy, 37*(10), 1001-1027.

Walsh, F. (1993). *Normal Family Processes, 2nd ed.* New York: Guilford.

Weick, A. (1983). Issues in overturning a medical model of social work practice. *Social Work, 28*(6), 467-471.

Weinstein, A., Feldtkeller, B., Malizia, A., Wilson, S., Bailey, J., & Nutt, D. J. (1998). Integrating the cognitive and physiological aspects of craving. *Journal of Psychopharmacology, 12*(1), 31-38.

Werner, E. E. (1989). Children of the Garden Island. *Scientific American, 260*(4), 106-111.

Wright, J. H., & Beck, A. T. (1983). Cognitive therapy of depression: Theory and practice. *Hospital and Community Psychiatry, 34*(12), 1119-1127.

Zastrow, C., & Kirst-Ashman, K. K. (1997). *Understanding Human Behavior and the Social Environment, 4th ed.* Chicago: Nelson-Hall.

SPECIAL TOPICS

Fear of Neuroscience:
A Dialogue About Social Work Practice
in the Addictions

Jerry Flanzer
E. Michael Gorman
Richard T. Spence

Moderator: Richard T. Spence

Moderator: It was suggested during the invitational Summit on Social Work and the Neurobiology of Addictions that there is a significant source of resistance to incorporation of neuroscience into social work theory and practice generally, and in addiction services in particular. That resistance is based on fears that a neurobiological focus will negate social work's traditional emphases on social environment, interpersonal relationships, and psychological con-

---

Jerry Flanzer, DSW, MSW, is Social Science Analyst, Services Research Branch, National Institute on Drug Abuse, Rockville, MD. E. Michael Gorman, PhD, MPH, MSW, is Assistant Professor of Social Work, San Jose State University, San Jose, CA. Richard T. Spence, PhD, MSSW, is Research Scientist and Director, Addiction Technology Transfer Center, University of Texas at Austin, School of Social Work.

[Haworth co-indexing entry note]: "Fear of Neuroscience: A Dialogue About Social Work Practice in the Addictions." Flanzer, Jerry, E. Michael Gorman, and Richard T. Spence. Co-published simultaneously in *Journal of Social Work Practice in the Addictions* (The Haworth Social Work Practice Press, an imprint of The Haworth Press, Inc.) Vol. 1, No. 3, 2001, pp. 103-112; and: *Neurobiology of Addictions: Implications for Clinical Practice* (ed: Richard T. Spence, Diana M. DiNitto, and Shulamith Lala Ashenberg Straussner) The Haworth Social Work Practice Press, an imprint of The Haworth Press, Inc., 2001, pp. 103-112. Single or multiple copies of this article are available for a fee from The Haworth Document Delivery Service [1-800-342-9678, 9:00 a.m. - 5:00 p.m. (EST). E-mail address: getinfo@haworthpressinc.com].

cepts and replace them with a mechanistic technologically based science. To what extent is this fear realistic?

Flanzer: Apparently, many social workers have dropped the "bio" in the original biopsychosocial approach fostered by our professional founders. In my experience in assessing the "whole person in situation," few social workers actually look at the health/mind-body connection. What is so exciting is that our–Mary Richmonds', Grace Coyle's, Bertha Reynolds'–understanding of the dynamic, reciprocal, influential effect of the environment, of interpersonal relationships, psychological/ego processes and biology/"brain wiring" on the social human being is being substantiated by science daily.

The ongoing research in substance abuse and mental illness illustrate this so well. For with modern technology, we can now see changing and improving brain patterns based on nurturing environmental changes. There is even the hint of research showing improving, responsive brain patterns due to "counseling."

Ultimately, the consideration of neurobiological status becomes an important part of diagnosis and treatment planning in the addictions. Substance abusers manifest behavioral abnormalities in addition to the compulsive self-administration of drugs of abuse. Such abnormalities, which apparently reflect underlying brain dysfunction, must be considered when one designs therapeutic interventions, especially those based on cognition or insight, or when asking a client to perform a decision making task. There are several neurological considerations in the treatment process.

- Physical deficits in brain function of drug abusers suggest that they may have problems in implementing cognitive strategies in therapy.
- Resistance of drug abuse problems to cognitive therapeutic approaches may reflect physical problems–not just that the client is "difficult."
- Motivation and timing of intervention can be clearly linked to the brain's readiness to receive and process input.
- Environmental trauma affects brain processes and development, which in turn shapes environmental and individual functioning.

In response to the "mechanistic" issue–I see that as a "smokescreen." I believe there is a future for noninvasive brain-imaging approaches that can be useful in learning about the ongoing neurobiology of the effect of an individual's drug abuse, abstinence, and treatment, not as an "end-all," but as a tool for decision making and action.

An important by-product of the "bio" psychosocial approach is the reinvigorating of a holistic course of action which would link organizational and financial services to all facets of the presenting problem.

Gorman: Jerry raises some good points, namely that of the "bio" in bio-psychosocial. It is true and not infrequently the case that the biological dimension gets left out of social work education and practice, or at least not sufficiently addressed.

But, to play devil's advocate for a moment, I think that these concerns about a "neurobiological focus," or about too much of a shift in that direction, are not entirely unfounded. I think this is the case, potentially, at several levels, and from a resources point of view from the perspective of managed care as well as from the perspective of research and policy priorities. Let me explain. It is not so simple to just say, "We'll pay more attention to the biological aspect(s) of addiction." The success of addiction treatment (i.e., interventions) has not been universally accepted, despite considerable scientific evidence to that fact and much rhetoric. Biology or no biology, there remain deep seated and firmly held ideological convictions that addiction is a moral problem, pure and simple, and that no amount of "treatment" is going to make any difference. Attitudes may be changing somewhat as recent election results in the western US may indicate (e.g., mandatory drug treatment in California for early offenders and medical use of marijuana in a few states) but for many, addiction is a moral problem, a "sin."

Social work by its very nature is engaged in working with individuals who exhibit very complex addictive behaviors which require considerable skill to ameliorate. All of which is to say, that in this era of quick fixes, there is well-founded concern that the proverbial baby could be thrown out with bathwater, even if there is no baby yet. If there does come a time when there is something resembling a neurobiological "magic bullet," a belief is that then therapy, practice, and/or intervention at whatever level–individual, family, group, community–is going to get short shrift no matter how much sense it makes, no matter how much scientific evidence there may be to support it. And I think in many social workers' minds, there is the suspicion that if the biological becomes too imperative, then that could spell serious problems for other social aspects of this admittedly complicated array of issues we subsume under the rubric of addiction and addiction intervention. Look at mental health. No one denies the tremendous contribution of advances in the treatment of mental health. Yet there are people just taking pills who should also have the benefit of other treatment modalities. We have all seen it happen, and in this era of managed care, the bottom line, like it or not, often becomes THE standard of practice, not in every case, but often enough to give us pause and serious second thoughts.

What I am saying is that at the practice level there might well be concern about too heavy a reliance on "neuroscience" without due consideration of its consequences. That may not be fair to neuroscience, but I think there is the lurking suspicion that other core aspects of what social workers do might get pushed aside, de-prioritized, and not seen as viable strategies if everything is understood in terms of a bunch of chemicals reacting in somebody's brain.

I think one might also voice a concern from the point of view of research and science policy. The history of the National Institutes of Health has been understandably a biomedical one, and in recent decades the emphasis on the "biological" as opposed to the "social" has been preeminent. In fact, one could argue that the biomedical frame of reference is a fairly dominant one, which can be very narrowly focused to the exclusion of what some might consider perfectly legitimate science, and especially social science. A focus inclusive of biological as well as behavioral domains may be harder to manage, but would be better science.

In this light, we are talking about research politics and, frankly, where you put your money, what your priorities are, and how you justify them. In recent years, *some might argue,* we are finally getting some decent levels of funding for social science, and perhaps as a corollary of that, better social science. This has occurred in part as more openness has crept into the understanding of what science is. I think the challenges of the HIV/AIDS epidemic were a catalyst for changes in some of that process. The exigencies of the HIV/AIDS crisis forced new thinking. This is especially seen in the kinds of issues that are of paramount concern to social workers. By putting too much re-emphasis on neuroscience, we could short-change other critical areas of social scientific endeavor such as funding for clinical and community studies in addictions treatment and prevention.

Then, of course, there is the whole debate about whether social science is somehow not only too "soft" but too "political" and depending on a given administration's priorities, legitimate social science research could be "discounted" in favor of more "neutral" biology.

Moderator: A second fear expressed in the discussions at the conference is that the concept of addiction as a genetically predisposed brain disorder identifies addicts as defectives. It precludes any meaningful ability of the person to change and any meaningful role for treatment to help bring about such change. How would you respond to this concern?

Flanzer: We are all genetically predisposed to something. Would one say that an individual is defective if he/she has a predisposition to another brain or neurological disorder–such as Alzheimer's disease, brain cancer, Parkinson's disease or multiple sclerosis? The onset of addiction begins with the voluntary act of taking drugs, no matter whether there is a genetically predisposed brain disorder or not. The continued repetition of voluntary drug taking begins to change into involuntary drug taking, ultimately to the point that the behavior is driven by a compulsive craving–a condition having to do with changes in brain function due to the prolonged drug use.

When does that "switch" flip from abuse to involuntary dependence? We do not know. It is different for different people. Treatment has proven to be effective for all categories of people with alcohol and other drug problems–the point is that predisposed does not mean hopeless. In fact, it may mean that science may have a new tool to help in differential diagnosis and treatment.

Whether an individual is predisposed or not, four major hypotheses (described by Jill Littrell in this volume) have been formulated to address the issue of why some people develop compulsive use patterns for particular drugs:

1. Drugs which are abused stimulate the brain's pleasure centers.
2. Drugs which are abused sensitize the motivational systems of the brain such that behavioral routines for acquisition of the drug are programmed, although activation of motivational systems is not necessarily pleasurable.
3. People who abuse drugs are naturally in an aversive state which drug use enables them to escape.
4. Drugs of abuse are associated with aversive withdrawal phenomena that can be elicited by conditioned stimuli. Thus, persons with drug use histories take drugs to avert withdrawal states.

Gorman: Once again, Jerry makes some very valid points. But by the same token I think there is the concern that such an approach could possibly complicate one's way of dealing with the problem even further by laying an additional layer of stigma on the individual. This is a problem not only with respect to addiction, but also with the tremendous increases in biological knowledge about any genetic condition that could have implications for treatment of any kind. In short, I think there are genuine ethical considerations with respect to not only this kind of diagnosis and its biomedical dimensions but also to what happens in turn to that information, i.e., who gets to control it.

Along the lines of Jerry's discussion, but giving it a somewhat different "spin," we know that substance abuse or dependence is stigmatized already. As I noted above, that stigma contributes to judgments about resources allocated to deal with the problem and judgments about whether "treatment" might be viable. Another concern is the tendency to "over-medicalize" the problem and view it exclusively in biological terms and ignore relevant environmental issues, or deprioritize them. There might be less of a tendency to view the problem holistically, i.e., in terms of the person-in-environment. While I do not think we are near to being able to pinpoint with accuracy what biological basis or genetic substrate might exist for most specific substance abuse problems, no matter how much information has exploded, there is the fear that further down the road we could be setting ourselves up for some Orwellian scenario such as using such information to label a category of people to their disadvantage. THAT prospect is a scary one.

Implicit here is an understanding of what addiction is and how it should be understood. In that regard, there are significant stakeholders, players and constituencies at the public policy table. Those individuals decide how resources are to be prioritized and allocated. Unfortunately, some at that table hold the view that addiction is a moral problem. And the perspectives of neuroscience could be used either to challenge or to support that concept. An individual with an addiction problem could be considered permanently "impaired" or "flawed." And while neuroscience research will continue to grow regardless of people's concerns, I think that many social workers and many other providers, researchers, ethicists, and others have genuine concerns about how the findings of neuroscience are utilized.

Again, I think there are parallels with mental health. No one would argue that neuroscience has made amazing contributions to the amelioration of mental health problems–schizophrenia, bipolar disorders, and depression to mention only a few. And it is the case that the "disease" model of mental illness has both allowed for these developments and contributed to the general destigmatization of mental health problems that has occurred over the last few decades. I say contributed, however, because the social reform movement that co-occurred was every bit as important in contributing to that process.

Something similar could occur with addiction, although I think we have a much longer road to go and perhaps a more difficult one. No one, no social worker, is going to oppose knowledge that contributes to more successful intervention, better care, and more humane treatment of individuals and a concomitant reduction in human suffering. The question is, ultimately, what is the role of neuroscience in this enterprise and how can the findings and insights be harnessed in a realistic manner to achieve social work goals, as opposed to making social work and social workers mere functionaries of a more narrowly focused biological imperative.

One final point. I think what is missing from the neuroscience debate thus far is a framework for viewing neurobiology in the larger scope of social work and allied health professions. What I see lacking in the proponency of neuroscience is a public health dimension. How does neuroscience, and for that matter social work interventions, modalities, etc., relate, and how might they be subsumed in some sort of framework that encompasses both?

I propose that public health, with its concern with person, place and time, the ecological perspective that it shares with social work, and its specification of primary (i.e., outreach, education), secondary (screening, assessment), and tertiary prevention (interventions, treatment, referral, linkages) may offer a way to synthesize and integrate both salient aspects of neuroscience with social work values, perspectives and methods. From my point of view, such a framework might be beneficial and might address limitations of both areas.

While social work emphasizes and acknowledges ecological and environmental perspectives, this view is narrowly focused with respect to the historically important social work practice fields, i.e., mental health, health, and child welfare, without seeing the bigger picture. In fact, in today's world, the interface of mental health and substance abuse services, health care, public welfare, and the range of social work modalities would seem to call out for some more overarching system that should draw on biology to accomplish its mission successfully. I think it can be said that social work, i.e., social work education, including continuing education, could benefit from better and more rigorous grounding in not only biology but also related public health science such as epidemiology. How many MSW students and practitioners really comprehend the implications of important epidemiological information for their general practice and particularly for their work in the addictions?

By the same token, what I see lacking on the neuroscientific side of the equation is precisely how that knowledge–insight–is related to CONTEXT. Context is another way of acknowledging the reality of environment. Whatever may be happening inside the brain, that reality is not the ONLY one. The meaning of contextual occurrences, both for the individual and his/her family and community, is of equal import.

In this respect, the experience of the HIV/AIDS epidemic and its science with respect to substance abuse (and especially drug abuse) offers some illustrations relevant to this discussion. This experience offers important object lessons for understanding how potentially antithetical perspectives can be brought to bear on a public health problem. Without going into great detail, suffice it to say that initially the problems of HIV/AIDS and drug abuse were subsumed under a traditional, biomedical, individualistic paradigm. This paradigm tended to classify all drug abusers under one sociological category (injection drug users or "IDUs") and often focusing interventions at the individual level. The problem was, and remains, that most IDUs and other substance users are OUTSIDE the traditional treatment arena.

HIV/AIDS was in fact a catalyst for some very radical changes in the way both drug users were understood–at both an individual and a collective level–and in terms of how their drug use related to the rest of their lives and their families. It became very clear, for example, that no matter how much one understood about heroin's actions on the brain (and the rest of the body), however successful methadone was in alleviating symptoms of heroin withdrawal and providing a safer medical alternative, that this biological knowledge and the "magic bullet " (some might say) of methadone have not solved the problem. Why? Because drug abuse, in this case, heroin, must be understood in terms of a considerable complex of behaviors and environmental and other personal factors. This fact has implications not only for treatment in the traditional sense, but also for prevention and outreach. In short, a problem that was once viewed somewhat uni-dimensionally is now understood to be a much more complex array of issues, which includes neuroscience, but which also includes all of the traditional tasks in which social work and social workers have been engaged. And as things moved further along, the awareness that not only neuroscience, and not only psychology [social work's favorite paradigm] but also anthropology and sociology, and pioneering work of social work researchers who utilized these more ecologically informing disciplines, were critical in developing the public health response to this problem.

Flanzer: Mike's response makes it clear that neuroscience and social work must be addressed in the context of sociopolitical realities. He correctly points out the existing problems posed by the "moral" and disease models, the politics of allocating scientific research money, and the need to place the neuroscience, the "bio" in context–that is, into day-to-day reality. I also interpret that much of what Mike is saying occurs because of different "terminology," jargon if you will, between the neuroscience (i.e., NIH) and social work education communities. For example, neuroscience emphasizes drug abuse as a brain disease acting upon and being effected by learned behavior, and social work refers to drug abuse as a result of a confluence of biopsychosocial factors.

Social work has been fighting against "the moral" model since the inception of the profession. Jane Addams and others fought the idea that people were poor because of their immorality and that rich people were inherently smarter and more moral. It took the Great Depression of the 1930s to strengthen the social work position. It has taken the AIDS epidemic and the drug epidemic to turn the moral issue around in a similar way for the overwhelming majority of the population. It is amazing how the morality issue quickly drops out when the disease gets close to home. As Mike notes, the AIDS epidemic has been one of the major forces to turn the public health agenda around by looking not only at technical concerns, but by also blending the "hard" and "soft" of neuroscience and social science. Research supported by the National Institute on Drug Abuse (NIDA) and the National Institute on Mental Health (NMH), and also at the National Cancer Institute (NCI), the National Institute on Aging (NIA), and elsewhere has repeatedly shown that "biological findings" alone do not lead to treatment breakthroughs. Furthermore, they also found that treatment interventions must have a social component to work in the real world. To put it another way, no medicine is found to work without an appropriate matching strategy for treatment delivery, and a social support component to sustain it. Mike correctly fears that were we to find a "morning-after pill" that would nullify the effects of the substance abuse, or if we found a genetic modification method to alter substance abuse effects, we would find those who rely on the pill only, but they would eventually fail because this medical response has no social component. NIDA is in the midst of promising clinical-pharmacological trials. We may have approved prescribed drugs that help people abstain, block or lose the compulsion or obsession to use. Would Mike say, stop working on these medication approaches because they might be misused or over-relied upon?

Forty years ago, Charles Perrow of the University of Wisconsin in his article, "A Framework for Comparative Organizational Analysis" (1976, *American Sociological Review*, 32, 194-208), referred to the power of money and resources leading to a plethora of information in a given scientific area–sometimes to the detriment of the advancement of science in other areas. Following his thinking, the mushroom of money for mental health interests led to more people being trained in mental health, which led to more mental health journals, which led to more reported findings, which led to more people wanting to go into the field, which led to a wider and wider definition of social and other problems as mental health ones. As a bi-product, more and more social workers chose work in mental health, redefining social work issues as mental health ones. Extending that logic, if you saw something as a substance abuse problem, you could not get funding or get published, but, if you reframed your concerns to conform to a mental health problem, you could get published, funded and/or reimbursed for your services. Now, due to a confluence of reasons, more and more money is pouring into substance abuse problems. Suddenly everything is an addiction. Suddenly a new era of research is funded and social workers are reimbursed for chemical dependency treatment services. Extending this argument further, now that substance abuse is being researched as a system problem, the focus is moving increasingly away from the individual and towards the family, the group. Problems of child welfare, violence, and emotional disorders suddenly have a substance abuse link. And social workers are specializing in substance abuse, and more group work and community work is being done in this area. Now even the brain and genetics can be viewed as a group and family inheritance issue–not an individual one. If this trend continues, increasingly, the link between the brain and the family and society, the distinction between the "bio"and the "social" will continue to blur. And social work will be the profession in the pivotal position to address the problem.

Gorman: Once again, Jerry points out several important considerations which inform the question at hand. The point about what happened in mental health may be especially salient in that it is possible a similar trajectory might someday occur in substance abuse. We are not there yet, but this possibility may represent a goal that might serve to reframe the future of alcohol and drug abuse services. In any case, Jerry argues, and I do not disagree with him, that neuroscience has a role to play in that reframing. I also think that the process may eventually facilitate improved success and efficacy in interventions as well as a more robust rationale for prevention, an area that we have not addressed in this conversation and which might merit greater consideration in this volume.

But to return to Dick Spence's initial question, namely, whether fears that a neurobiological focus will negate social work's traditional emphases on social environment, interpersonal relationships, and psychological concepts; and replace them with a mechanistic technologically based science are realistic, the answer remains equivocal. But that very conclusion has implications for a continuing dialogue on these questions.

On the one hand, the advance of neuroscience will continue and will influence not only the way that clients are treated and with what medications, but also the way in which the question of addiction itself is understood. Social workers need to be cognizant of this social fact and its implications for policy, i.e., resource allocation and prioritizations. Simply digging in one's heels or, to use another metaphor, sticking one's head in the proverbial sand, will not make neuroscience less relevant to social work practice, education or policy.

By the same token, neuroscience, in and of itself, does not and will not have all the answers to this very complex set of issues. We need to remain aware of this limitation, particularly with respect to environmental, i.e., ecological and systems approaches. There is resistance on the part of many neuroscientists to the concepts of ecology and environment and to the findings of contemporary social science. These concepts are often dismissed as "soft" or irrelevant, by at least some scientists. But as the HIV/AIDS experience has reminded us, changing human behavior can be daunting. Even with medications that "work," the challenges of "adherence" remain considerable as any social worker working with HIV positive and at-risk populations can attest.

At the end of the day, I think that while social workers may understandably be concerned about the incorporation of neuroscience and its implications for social work practice in the addictions, it is nonetheless imperative for social workers to have an understanding of neuroscience and its implications. If a paradigm shift is occurring under the rubric of "addiction," there is also one occurring in social work, that educators, researchers *as well as practitioners* must heed if the profession is to establish a more commanding presence at the science and health policy table. For this to happen, it will be necessary for social workers to educate themselves better in this area, not only so as to improve their ability to incorporate relevant findings in their research, practice, and teaching, but also to be better able to speak the same language as their colleagues in the public health and biological sciences. Professional development will include neuroscience and public health knowledge as well as more rigorous training in the social sciences and identification of the implications of these fields for social work practice. If social work and social workers do their homework, the profession will be that much better positioned to speak from the strengths of its experience and convincingly articulate and advocate for the complementarity of the profession's ecological and systems perspectives.

Index

AA (Alcoholics Anonymous), 14-15, 34,90. *See also* TSF (twelve-step facilitation)
Abortions, spontaneous, 47-48
Acamprosate, 16,66-67,74-76
Acetadehyde, 17
Acetylcholine, 11,15
ADD (Attention Deficit Disorder), 30-34,51-52
Addiction, causes of
  introduction to, 1-8,20-21
  neurobiologic causes
    brain chemistry, 11-12
    emotional learning, 13-14
    genetics, 10-11
    sensitization, 11-13
  non-drug therapies for, 14-15
  pharmacotherapies for
    alcohol dependence therapies, 16-18
    comparative listings of, 16
    detoxification therapies, 16-17
    heroin dependence therapies, 16, 19-20
    introduction to, 1-6,15-16
    nicotine dependence therapies, 16,20
    psychostimulant dependence therapies, 16,18-19
    relapse reduction therapies, 16-20
  reference literature about, 21-22
  SPAM (stigma, prejudice, and misunderstanding) and, 8
  terminology of, 8-10
Adjunctive drugs, 34-35
Adolescents, impact of AOD (alcohol and other drugs), 45,52-54

Adulthood, impact of AOD (alcohol and other drugs), 45,54-56
Alcohol abuse and addiction, 11-18, 30-35,41-48,54-59,65-78
Alcohol and other drugs (AOD), neurobiological aspects of. *See* AOD (alcohol and other drugs), neurobiological aspects of
Alcoholics Anonymous. *See* AA (Alcoholics Anonymous)
Amantadine, 16,18
American Psychiatric Association. *See* APA (American Psychiatric Association)
Amphetamine, 24
Anabolic steroids, 16
Antabuse, 16-17
Anticholinergics, 32
Antidepressants, 16,18,67
Anxiogenics, 26
AOD (alcohol and other drugs), neurobiological aspects of
  addiction, causes of, 7-22. *See also* Addiction, causes of
  brain, impact on
    ADD (Attention Deficit Disorder) and, 51-52
    adolescent stage, 45,52-54
    adulthood stage, 45,54-56
    brain plasticity, 41-42,44-46
    childhood stage, 45,49-52
    clinical practice and, 58
    FAS (Fetal Alcohol Syndrome) and, 49
    introduction to, 1-6,41-44
    life cycle stages and, 45-52
    neuronal functions *vs.* drug action brain sites, 43

SSOs (supportive significant others),
  69,73-74
SSRIs (serotonin reuptake inhibitors),
  90-91
Stanford-Binet Intelligence Scale, 49
Stimulants, 24,25
Stress and stress hormones, 25,50-51
Sucrose, 26
Supportive significant others. *See*
  SSOs (supportive significant
  others)
Symmetrel, 16,18

Talk therapy, 70
Tegretol, 16
Thorazine, 32
Tobacco. *See* Nicotine
Tranquilizers, 45
Trexan, 35
TSF (twelve-step facilitation), 14-16,
  20-21,67-69

Twelve-step facilitation. *See* TSF
  (twelve-step facilitation)

United States, Department of Health
  and Human Services, 82,94
University of Wisconsin, School of
  Social Welfare, 72,111

Valium, 17

Wilcox, Richard E., 7-22
Withdrawal symptoms, 88

Zofran, 16
Zweben, Allen, 3,65-80
Zyban, 16,20